Stories From The Couch

Stories From The Couch

◆

And Other Telling Tales

Mark S. Benn, Psy.D.

iUniverse, Inc.
New York Lincoln Shanghai

Stories From The Couch
And Other Telling Tales

Copyright © 2008 by Mark S. Benn

iUniverse books may be ordered through booksellers or by contacting:

iUniverse
2021 Pine Lake Road, Suite 100
Lincoln, NE 68512
www.iuniverse.com
1-800-Authors (1-800-288-4677)

Because of the dynamic nature of the Internet, any Web addresses or links contained in this book may have changed since publication and may no longer be valid.

The information, ideas, and suggestions in this book are not intended as a substitute for professional advice. Before following any suggestions contained in this book, you should consult your personal physician or mental health professional. Neither the author nor the publisher shall be liable or responsible for any loss or damage allegedly arising as a consequence of your use or application of any information or suggestions in this book.

ISBN: 978-0-595-47362-5 (pbk)
ISBN: 978-0-595-91640-5 (ebk)

Printed in the United States of America

For my Parents, my Children and Barbara

Contents

Preface

Over the course of the past twenty-five years I have spent countless hours listening to the stories of people's lives. It has been a remarkably privileged place to be and I have been honored with the opportunity to be invited into the private world of so many people. Spending my career as a psychologist has been difficult, exciting, interesting, scary, confusing and rich; one thing it has never been is boring. People are fascinating and if you were to fill the biggest stadium in the world with hundreds of thousands of people, they'd all have one thing in common—they would all have problems. Problems with identity, meaning in life, their parents, their children, their romantic relationships, their jobs; people struggle with money, abuse, fidelity, teachers, spirituality, prejudice, poverty, addiction and death. As a psychologist my job has been to be there for people while they struggle with these common afflictions. I have learned that, while many people want a solution to their problems, most simply want someone to hear them, to understand them and to be there to offer guidance.

Through the course of my work I have found that it is helpful to use metaphors and pictures to illustrate the common themes and struggles that people deal with in their lives. Often, it is as if I am sitting in the passenger seat in a car as clients drive through their life stories; I get to point things out along the way that they may have missed because they're so intent on driving. At other times in my life, I have been the one who was blindly driving, and I have relied on my family, friends, and even clients to help me see the road.

This book is a collection of vignettes about some of the most common themes in people's lives. The names and identifying features of my clients have been changed to protect their identities, and some of the characters in these vignettes are a composite of many people I have seen over my years of practice. Many of the themes I see in the lives of my clients are also reflected in my own life, and so I included personal stories as well. My hope is that you will find yourself or someone you love in these stories and the pages that follow. Perhaps by reading this book you will learn something that will help you navigate the road you travel— and in doing so may you make peace with your story and your life

1

Watch Out For That Tree

I recall watching the television show "Bewitched" when I was young and seeing the *normalcy* with which Samantha would meet Darren at the door with a martini. Every time Larry Tate came over, he and Darren would have a drink. It's just the way things were in America, in the 1970s. So it was not terribly unusual when Mark Wodyka's father came home drunk one night and smashed his car into a good-sized tree in our neighborhood. It was, of course, big news at the bus stop the next day and we were relieved he wasn't hurt. The tree also survived the crash. But Mr. Wodyka and the tree were bruised. Mark's dad took a few stitches in the head while the tree got a tremendous notch taken out, about four feet from its base, where the car bumper had bitten into it.

Throughout my childhood, I must have driven by that tree hundreds of times. The tree was, and still is, located on the small parkway between the home I grew up in on Chestnut Lane and the main road leading to the bus stop. Everybody had to drive by that tree to get home. Over the years I got to see that tree grow and with it, the scar of the accident. It expanded and changed, a constant reminder of Mr. Wodyka's accident. The tree's scar gave it a shape none of the other trees had. The blemish altered the tree, changing how it grew and looked forever. David Bowie sings, *"I watch the ripples change their size but never leave the stream ..."* That's how the accident affected that

1

tree. People are like that too: affected by events that occur and left with scars—both visible and invisible. These events impact us in some way and forever change who (and how) we are, but never leave the *stream* that we are.

As a very young boy, perhaps six or seven, I thought my chin looked funny. One day, as I looked in the mirror and seriously examined my face, I lifted my neck and stretched the skin to see why my face looked wrinkled. I saw the spot where I'd had stitches when I was two after a fall into the corner of a table. I had never noticed this so well before. I didn't like what I saw and I spent a good deal of my adolescent years alternating between pretending it wasn't there and hating it for altering my face.

One night my 11-year-old son, Andrew, was playing wall ball with two of his best friends, Ryan and Steven. I was not surprised when Steven came in to tell me that Ryan and Andrew had been mean to him and that he wanted to go home. Ryan and Andrew couldn't understand why Steven was *so* upset. But he was and he wanted to go home. I asked the three boys to go inside and try to talk it out. They did this with enough success that Steven stayed and they went back to their game. Later that night, Andrew asked me what had upset Steven so much. He hadn't seen the conflict as any big deal but saw that Steven got *very* upset and was hard to console. It was clear that the time had come to tell Andrew about Mr. Wodyka's run-in with the tree. You see, Steven's father died suddenly, less than a year ago, at the age of 43. Andrew knew this and had been incredibly moved by the event. I explained to Andrew that, like the tree, Steven would never be quite the same. He would grow and be altered forever by the trauma of his loss at such a young age. The loss would affect Steven, just as the events that happen to each of us change who (and how) we are. We could see how Mr. Wodyka's accident had changed the tree. It is clearly visible even 25 years after the accident. The same is true

for Steven. Except his *"accident"* would be largely invisible as it had
been during the game of wall ball.

Steven's tears that night over a "minor" event in a kid's game may
have had more to do with his father's death than with what actually
happened during the game. Andrew seemed to understand this and
added that Steven would be moving in the next few months. That
meant coming over to play would no longer be as simple as hopping
on his bike. This too may have led to Steven's sadness.

We've all had cars metaphorically run into the trunks of our trees. I
know I have. My parents' divorce when I was five comes to mind
immediately. It left a scar and taught me a lot. Some of the lessons
have helped me. Others are simply reminders of hurts that I still don't
understand. I doubt the tree knows why it is so different. But it is.
Steven probably doesn't know why certain things hurt him so deeply.
But they still hurt. No matter how long Steven (or you or I) live and
grow, the scars left from the traumas of our lives will affect and shape
us into who we become in this life. And if we are lucky, we will continue to grow, like the tree, in spite of our traumas.

Look at the scars you carry through life. Honor them for what they
have taught you and try to let go of the pain that created them.
Andrew may be able to see how the unfortunate death of Steven's
father can be a lesson. Someday, perhaps Steven will see it too. What
can you see when you look at the scars you have (both visible and
invisible) from the cars that have run into (and scarred) the tree that is
you?

2

Who Am I? Who Are You?

I just loved the way Tim Gilliland's handwriting looked. He had this really neat way of writing his E's. The three lines were barely connected to each other, they were just three horizontal dashes, and no vertical line holding them together ... it was very cool.

So I stole it. Yep, I stole Tim Gilliland's E, made it my own. I often wonder what his E looks like today. I don't think he ever even knew I took it; I wasn't going to tell him.

Somewhere in his book, <u>Something Happened</u>, Joseph Heller says, *"Even my handwriting's not my own."* I could really relate to that. I recall feeling scared when I read that, scared Tim Gilliland would find out. More importantly though, I got scared there were *other* things that weren't really mine that made me an impostor. I started to think of all the times people had told me I looked like my dad, that I laugh like my mother, that *"I was definitely a Benn!"* My kids are told that too. I wonder if that robs them of an identity or gives them one.

Thinking back on it now, I wonder who I really am. Is there anything that is uniquely mine? Is there even such a thing as an original thought? Damn, I don't even like thinking that to type it. It's scary. No wonder I have an identity crisis, often wondering what I really think, feel, and believe. Often, I am curious about who and how I want to be. Am I really a Democrat or is that what my parents were? What parts of me are really mine and what parts are the sums of the other people whom I have known? Are all the parts of me borrowed characteristics and traits, like I borrowed Tim Gilliland's letter E?

In many self-help books the reader is told to *"know yourself."* Essentially we are told, "to thine own self be true." But who is my own self? How do I figure that out? What if I am not sure who I am and how I got to be this way?

When I was younger I thought I knew what I wanted in life. As I get older, I wonder if the things I think I want are really the dreams of my family, my religion, my culture or my society. Happiness seems to elude so many people who are not sure what they want. How can one be sure what one wants, when one is not even sure of who one is?

People often come to therapy to find out *who they are.* They end up sitting and talking to other people (who may not know who *they* are) in an attempt to solve issues or find direction in life. It almost sounds like "the blind leading the blind." (I am reminded of a woman facilitator at a workshop who asked, "Who better to lead the blind, than other blind people?")

I hear people ask things like, "When will I know who I am and be comfortable with that?" My answer is always the same: "I don't know the answer to that for me. How could I know for you?"

This journey is one some have called "an existential crisis." I conceptualize this to mean that you must essentially "strip away" all of the things that you are not and leave the parts that truly are you. The danger here is that after the *striping away* there will be nothing of your own left, not even your handwriting. This is no simple task, and it is definitely a scary one to pursue.

I picture this process like peeling back the layers of paint or wallpaper that have been applied to my soul. Like stripping away, layer after layer, the colors or paper that have been brushed and put onto my face, my body and my spirit. Who am I? Who are you? What do I think? What do I value and what do I have to do to figure this out?

Often, in therapy, I will challenge people to examine where they are going in life and explore if this is what *THEY* truly want or if this is something that they think others expect or hope for them. I too, examine this while we talk and share my own struggles about how I have suffered and plodded my way through this journey. I will share about my handwriting and how I have borrowed and given back certain things that I thought I wanted and kept some of the things, ideas, goals, dreams and aspirations that I have had. This is a scary, wonderful and essential journey to find out who we are, what we want and how to get there. Embracing this struggle, staring right at it and finding someone you trust to explore this with will surely help you get on track as you peel back the layers, take off the wallpaper, and scrape the paint as you attempt to see who you really are.

Sometimes I think that my handwriting never was very good, and I wonder if it's because it isn't really mine.

3

Try This

Randle Patrick McMurphy wanted to get out of the psychiatric ward where he was incarcerated in the Milos Forman film based on Ken Kesey's book, <u>One Flew Over the Cuckoo's Nest</u>. In one memorable scene in the movie, McMurphy takes bets that he can lift a sink off the floor and throw it out the window and escape to freedom. After failing to do so he screams at the other patients on the ward: "But I tried, didn't I? Goddamnit, at least I did that!"

He tried, at least he tried. Do you try? Can you? Will you? Will I? It seems to me that the honorable and noble thing to do in this life is to try, not to quit, not to constantly retreat to safety, but to try. It's scary, trying. Actually, it's not the trying that is so scary. It's the possibility of failing—that's what freaks us out and keeps us from attempting to go where we want to go and do what we dream to do.

At its core, that's what my book is about: trying and dreaming, taking the risk to fail or succeed. There's no way to know in advance if the risks are worth what you will receive for your efforts. It is also not true that if you just try hard enough you will succeed and get what you want. You may not, but as R.P. McMurphy suggests, *"At least I tried."* There is a lot of peace to be had in trying.

Sandra is a 23-year-old woman whose ancestry is Turkish. Her skin is darker than a White person's, but not as dark as a black person's. No one in her family made it past high school in their educational pursuits. When Sandra was 19 she met Nicholas, got pregnant with Michael, and at 21 she had Chad. Sandra and Nicholas were poor, living on some assistance while Nicholas worked hard at a local factory to make ends meet. Sandra wanted more in life than to go month to month financially, so she enrolled in the local community college, found other women to "co-op" babysit with her kids, and began taking classes. Nicholas wanted to work, come home, play video games and have Sandra do the rest—so she did.

Sandra's father committed suicide when she was twelve. Her family life growing up was unstable, to say the least. She wanted stability. She was willing to do anything to get stability, except give up her dreams of making a better life for herself and her new family. This scared Nicholas; he didn't think he could keep up with Sandra and this led him away from Sandra. Eventually, Nicholas decided he wanted something more in his life too. But what he wanted didn't include Sandra or their two sons.

Sandra was very sad and came in to talk about what *she* had done wrong. What had Sandra done?

Mikey grew up in a town where everyone played sports. Playing sports was the thing to do. Mikey was very short for his age—so were his parents—and he probably wasn't going to grow very tall. So what sport did Mikey pick to play? He picked basketball, of course. He played and he played and he played. He'd go down to the playground and he'd stand around until a team was one player short and he got picked. He was almost always the last one chosen. In eighth grade Mikey tried out for his junior high school basketball team and made the team; he rarely played in games, but he was on the team. Mikey kept trying. He went out for the team again in ninth grade, and got cut. He continued playing and went out for the team again in tenth grade, only to be cut again. This devastated Mikey, especially when the coach told him he was good enough, just that he was too short. This was little consolation to Mikey.

By the time eleventh grade rolled around, Mikey was uncertain about his desire to go out for the team—after all, he hadn't played since eighth grade, and then, he hadn't played much. Mikey tried out anyway, made the team, and became the starting point guard. His team was awful, losing almost every game by a huge margin. In twelfth grade, Mikey was ready for his team to be successful and he was ready to be the team's starting point guard again. Mikey made the team, became the starting guard again, and broke his wrist two games into the season.

Sandra and Mikey tried. Things didn't come out the way they had dreamt, but they tried, dammit, at least they tried.

At the end of Forman's *Cuckoo's Nest*, R.P. McMurphy loses his battle too. The Chief, who has become one of McMurphy's best friends in the story, grabs that sink, lifts it off the ground and throws it through the wall. He runs through the hole in the wall to (what looks like) freedom. We never know what happens to the Chief ... we cannot know what will happen to Sandra, her sons, or her soon-to-be ex-husband. We can't even know what will happen to Mikey ... but we can guess.

My guess is, they kept on trying. People like Sandra, Mikey and the Chief will be successful. They will keep trying with mixed results; succeeding sometimes, failing others, but trying nonetheless. As I watch people in therapy it appears that the people who are most successful are NOT the ones who always succeed at *what* they do; they're the ones who keep trying regardless of *how* they do.

What I know for sure is that the only failure is in not trying. In trying, we have a chance at success; by not trying we have none.

4

Let's Go Clubbing

The Hair Club for Men. American Girls doll collectors. Fly Fishermen of America. The National Rifle Association. NASCAR. AFL-CIO. The American Cancer Society. And so on and so on. You name it, they have a club for it. Fan clubs, sports clubs, music clubs, climbing clubs, car clubs, motorcycle clubs, all kinds of clubs. I can hardly think of anything that doesn't have its own club.

One of the unique things about me is I have webbed toes. The second and third toes on each foot are stuck together, webbed. The toes on my right foot are more webbed than the toes on my left. A lot of people have toes like these. As a child I often wondered *how many* people had toes like mine. I wanted to start a "Webbed Toes Club of America." I even considered making a certificate and membership card of some sort and advertising for admission into this club. I figured if I could get people to send me $10 and a self-addressed stamped envelope, I could make a lot of money.

People must love and need to belong to something. How else can you explain the existence of so many clubs? With the creation of the Internet and e-mail, people are more connected to each other than ever. And yet, there are so many lonely people, people out searching for somewhere they belong. People seem to want someone to connect to, someone who understands them and has interests similar to theirs.

It seems clear that certain clubs attract certain kinds of people. People who share certain kinds of beliefs: politically, religiously, socially and in other ways. Look at the people who go to auto races for example. My guess is that people who go to NASCAR races listen to more country music than show tunes; and that people who belong to the Sierra Club listen to National Public Radio and are more likely to vote Democratic.

Like attracts like. We want to be around people who think and act like we do. There must be something comforting about that. There's less tension when you are around people who look like you, act like you and think like you. Even the kids in high school who want to be different hang around other kids in high school who want to be different. The bizarre looking, non-traditional types find themselves with other bizarre non-traditional types. The "preps" find themselves with preps, the jocks with jocks, the druggies with other druggies. Water seeks its own level; people do, too.

One of the most different looking groups today is the "Goth's" or gothic-looking kids. About a year ago I received a call from a woman who wanted to find a therapist. This mother called my office and said she wanted to get her teenage daughter in to therapy and was wondering if I could be of assistance. We agreed upon a time and the daughter agreed to come. The day before the session the mother called and said she wanted to *warn* me about her daughter. She wanted to warn me that her daughter "looked different." I didn't know what this meant, and I didn't ask. I simply said, "Fine," and assured her I would be prepared.

Actually, I was being casual about it. I couldn't imagine she would be *that* different. Well, I was wrong. This young woman was dramatically different looking. When I went to the waiting room of my practice, I was glad the mother had warned me. I still wasn't prepared for what I saw, but with the advanced warning, I was not totally shocked either. This young woman wore all black, flowing capes, veils, lipstick, nail polish and makeup. Her face was literally painted with black designs around her eyes, her cheeks and her mouth.

Lucky for me, as a psychologist I was trained never to look shocked at anything. We are never to drop our jaw in disbelief or bewilderment. If a client comes in and says they like to have sex while hanging from ceiling fans by bungee cords tied to their ankles, we are not to freak out. Our job is to stay calm and say, "Hmmm, tell me more."

With this woman, I wanted to know more. So, being the direct, provocative therapist I am, I asked. I asked her what was up with the face painting. She told me she had painted her face to shock people. She claimed she wanted to teach people a lesson. She went on to say that she was a straight A student and captain of the cheerleaders. She claimed that she only painted her face "Goth-like" three days a week. She told me that on these days certain students followed her down the halls and threatened to beat her up, for no other reason than her make-up. This brave young woman told me she was just trying to make a point to others and she was willing to put up with abuse to teach it.

Most of us have some kind of choice to make about which clubs we join. We tend to find clubs that will take us as members. We search for people who will help us feel comfortable about our interests and we often find comfort in people who have similar interests. Some people jump out of a "comfort zone" to join in something that is scary and dangerous just to make a point.

By the end of the session with this young "Goth" woman, I could tell nothing was *wrong* with her. It was clear that the only thing wrong was the environment in which she lived—an environment that didn't want to tolerate her (choice of) difference. This woman was fine, perfectly fine. She believed she had a mission in life, a job to do. She was no different really than the people in Amnesty International, the Young Republicans, or the NRA. She had a vision of belonging to a group that taught tolerance by forcing her peers to confront the fact that she could look different and still be the same person they accepted and admired on the days her face was unpainted.

I enjoyed this woman immensely. I appreciated her bravery and her message. Her club is welcome at my house anytime she wants to visit. I may not agree with all the things she believes, I may not want to do all the things she does, but that's no different than how I feel about most clubs where I am not a member.

By talking to this young woman I learned that we also shared some core values, and I could respect her choices even those I would not have made myself.

We all belong to clubs that others may use to label or judge us; my hope is that my toes do not offend you and that you won't want to threaten me because my toes are different from yours. Because if we can respect our differences we may even find places where our values and beliefs converge. So, tell me about your club and I'll tell you about mine.

Hell, for $10 and a self-addressed stamped envelope, I'll even let you join!

5

Mr. Blake

Compensatory behaviors are behaviors we engage in to compensate for some of our own limits or deficiencies. These limits can be either self-imposed or perceived, or they can be threats to our competence from teachers, parents, clergy, society, or others on the outside. I have always felt the need to compensate for being short. Whether it was my own perception that I was treated differently or that I was not seen as an equal didn't matter. It was clear (at least to me) that I had to find some way to compensate for being much shorter than the average male.

The way I compensated was not unlike many males who feel some-what incompetent; I looked to sports as a place to achieve. I looked to sports for other things too, to find good male role models and to be around boys who seemed to be like me. Finding myself competent in sports and being an athlete helped me to forget about those missing inches ... until I met Mr. Blake.

Let me be clear from the start. I hated Mr. Blake. To me, he has become symbolic of all the people who ever took delight in prodding me for weaknesses and then ridiculing me when I winced in response ... you know the type. You've probably had some of these people in your life too: the people you hate for the things they did to you, or maybe even just the things that you thought they did.

Mr. Blake kicked my ass. He was the 8th grade football coach who chided me, embarrassed me, poked me in the chest hard as hell and yelled at me in front of the entire football team, **"MR. BENN, GO SIT THIS PLAY OUT AND WATCH JOE KLINE RUN IT! HE KNOWS WHAT TO DO. WATCH THE PLAY, MR. BENN, UNTIL YOU LEARN IT!"** Mr. Blake scared me every day. He humiliated me in front of the entire team. He laughed at me with the other coaches and made me feel even smaller than I already felt. He turned 8th grade football into torture for me.

But I still went to practice every day. I went afraid, not of being hurt physically, but of being hurt inside. I was afraid I would be told I was a sissy (although "sissy" isn't the word my peers used). Being thought weak or stupid or cowardly was everyone's greatest fear in junior high, and the only thing worse than being a sissy was being a short sissy. So, I learned courage. I did exactly what Mr. Blake was trying to get me to do: I got tough. I learned the plays (even though I had to write them on my arm for the first game), I never forgot my mouthpiece, I got to practice on time and I worked my butt off. I worked so hard that by the time the first game came around, I was the starting half-back for my 8th grade football team. I was 15 pounds smaller than any other kid, but I was out there when the opening kick-off got booted.

Now, I'm guessing you think I am going to thank Mr. Blake for helping me to succeed, but that's not what this story is about. I worked hard and I was good. But that success was mine and mine alone, and I still hate what the man did. He was downright mean. (In psychology we often say that the bigger an ass someone is, the more pain they're probably in. Had I known that then, it may have been some consolation to me, but I doubt it.) Mr. Blake accomplished his goal, but he damaged the spirit of a 14-year-old boy who had loved football more than any of the other sports he used to compensate for being short.

Midway through the season I did something I was taught to never do: I quit the team. I had grown to hate football. Mr. Blake, in all his lying glory, told me I couldn't quit the team because he was cutting me! He wasn't going to let this little sissy get the best of him, of that he was certain. To this day, he probably still believes he helped mold the character of young men by being a tyrant. He grew up with an entire generation of men who thought that by being mean they could help build other men. Nothing could've changed the way Mr. Blake was and wishing for him to change would have been about as futile as wishing for extra inches I will never have.

I've known a lot of Mr. Blake's in my life: the English teacher in high school and my speech professor in college who gave me a 'C'; the graduate school professors who told me I didn't have what it takes to get an advanced graduate degree. They hurt me and put me down; the bully in 7th grade and the one in 11th grade; Brian who laughed at my fear and threatened to leave me alone in the street, the first time my crowd cut school together. Thinking back, I realize I've hated a lot of people who, for one reason or another, seemed to hate me. These are the people who never took the trouble to see who I was, who saw that I was short and assumed that I was also small: small in courage, small in heart, and small in spirit.

So early in my life I learned compensatory behaviors—a lot of them—and they've helped me to hold my head high when a Mr. Blake comes along. I've played a lot of sports, even after my experience with Mr. Blake, to look for men to mentor me and to be accepted like the big guys. I try to be funny to diffuse a tense situation and to make friends, because it's hard to dislike someone who makes you laugh. I worked hard in school because I didn't want people to think I was stupid. Compensatory behavior: behavior used to compensate for some perceived or real deficiency.

I've come to realize that these behaviors aren't just about hiding my insecurities from the world, but about making myself into the kind of person I want to be. And I feel more at peace now when I think of the bullies from my life, all of the people who told me in their own special way that I was no good, that I couldn't make it. They helped make me stronger although I will never sanction their methods—I think there are better ways. But what they taught me is that changing their opinion of me is not as important as pushing myself to become the person I would like to be. I have more power over my life than they do, and I am not going to let anyone else tell me who, what and how I am.

That is up to me. From now on, I will not allow them to define who I am. I will be who I want to be, and if another Mr. Blake comes around I will tell him that he cannot hurt me anymore.

6

Reflections

When I was growing up, birthdays were generally not a super big deal in my house like they are in many people's homes. As a result, it is always a stretch for me to get genuinely involved and excited about the birthdays in my house now. Jerry Seinfeld even makes jokes about the fact that we often go nuts in this country about birthdays when, to him, all birthdays really are saying is that you didn't die in the past twelve months. Kids see birthdays differently though. To kids, each birthday is supposed to be a big event.

In an attempt to be a better father I wanted to give Rachel a special birthday when she turned seven. We have a mini-tradition in our family where one of the parents takes the birthday child out to lunch or dinner alone to a restaurant of the child's choice. It's a nice idea and is given in addition to other gifts and a party of some sort.

Rachel was excited to have a chance to go out alone with her dad, to get dressed up and be the *special* one for a night. She had earned it. After all, she wasn't just the birthday girl, she was the fourth child and oldest daughter, and had been forced to share the limelight with her incredibly adorable two-year-old sister, Beth.

Rachel decided that she wanted to go to Young's, the most popular Vietnamese restaurant in town. It was also one of my favorite restaurants—at least it was when I first moved to this town. I really wasn't a big fan of Young's anymore, not because of the food, but because I was pretty tired of it. Young's was simply worn out; I had eaten there too many times and was mostly done eating there. But we decided on Young's as Rachel's choice; it was her birthday, and it was her choice.

So, off we went, and it was glorious: my seven year-old daughter and me. It was sweeter than candy. She looked so happy and adorable sitting across from me, smiling, eating her spring rolls (her favorite) and just being alone with her dad. We talked and laughed and held hands, we looked into each other's eyes and we felt like there was no one else in that restaurant but us. When we finished eating the server brought some of that amazing flaming ice cream, what a sight. This was the picture of happy.

When we finished eating I told Rachel that we could drive downtown to Nature's Own, the *New Age*-like store that sold the special rock earrings she had been wanting. She was surprised and ecstatic—me too, I had finally figured out this birthday thing. While there, we were told that not only could she have the earrings, but also the matching necklace, free with the purchase of the earrings. Life was great.

We drove home happy as could be, we held hands as we drove and continued to talk and love each other like only a father and daughter can. It was heaven on earth, a picture to hold in our memories forever.

Upon arriving home Rachel showed off her new earrings to her mother and said that she wanted daddy to put her to sleep. Her mother took one smell of us and said, "Did you eat curry tonight?" She was glad to let me put her to sleep; she was hoping that I'd fall asleep in Rachel's room too!

The nightly ritual for bedtime in our house is usually snack, bath, book, lying with each child (not the teenagers) and, if all goes well (ha ha), then sleep. On this night, I was certain that everything would be perfect. Rachel brushed her teeth, picked out a book, waited for me, and I read to her. Then, I turned out the light and began recapping the night with her. "Wasn't that great Rachel?" I said, "What a perfect night. I had so much fun, happy birthday honey, I love you, good night."

With that Rachel burst into tears, crying very loud, shocking the hell out of me and screamed, **"You love Beth more than you love me! You like her the best, she's your favorite!"** Now please understand, she actually said more than that, but I was so shocked I can't even remember what it was she said exactly. I was incredulous. How could she be saying that? My mind was going crazy. I wanted to say, "Are you out of you damn mind girl!? I just spent the entire night with you, took you to Young's—I am so sick of Young's—burnt my tongue on that stupid flaming ice cream, smell like garlic and have to wash with sandpaper just to get in bed with your mother! I took you downtown to Nature's Own for those stupid rock earrings that cost me twenty bucks and will probably end up stuck to a piece of gum under that seat of the van in less than a week, I read you a Berenstain Bears book I must've read a hundred and fifty freaking times, and now you tell me you think I love Beth more?! YOU ARE SUCH A SPOILED BRAT!"

Relax reader, that's not what I said, that's what I *wanted* to say ... the brain goes very fast, so I thought all that in less than five seconds; it probably took you longer to read it. I actually composed myself and said this: "Oh honey, that must be tough to see Beth get so much attention, two year-olds are so cute it must look like everybody loves her more."

With that, she cried even louder (which told me I hit the nail right on the head) and said, "Yeah, sometimes I just hate her."

I held Rachel tighter and rubbed her back until she stopped crying, which didn't take very long. I told her I loved her, to which she responded that she loved me too, and gently fell asleep. It was a perfect night, one to remember forever—but it almost wasn't.

There was a lesson here that takes time to learn. And one you will get to practice often: In times of emotional distress, when you REALLY disagree with what is being said to you, be certain to *reflect* and not *react*. Rachel just wanted to be heard; most people do, especially when they are in pain. I have learned that generally speaking, people don't want you to solve their problems; they just want you to hear them. The times it is most important to hear what another is saying seems to be when they are in some kind of emotional pain, as Rachel was on her seventh birthday. I vehemently disagreed with what she was saying, and this too is a lesson for me: It's even more important to reflect and not react defensively when you disagree with what you are hearing the other say. It is also the most difficult time to do so.

In therapy and in life it is most important to try to tell someone what you hear them saying, especially when you disagree with what you are hearing. The results are almost magical. Try it, you might be surprised at the result.

7

Get Ready

Carla didn't leave Lenny until she was ready. She tried, but she couldn't. She *knew* she should, but that didn't matter.

People never do anything until they are ready. Mitchell and Mark are twins; Mitchell learned to walk at nine months, Mark at sixteen months. Mark learned to talk at ten months; Mitchell didn't talk until he was two and a half.

Rita learned cursive writing by second grade. Andrew learned his times tables at nine. Jarad still doesn't know his. We learn to do things when we are ready to learn them, not before. We try to compare our learning style and speed to others; we try to compare our kids to the "norm." It doesn't matter.

Each of us is so unique it doesn't make much sense to compare, but we do. Comparing myself to others makes me feel inadequate more times than it makes me feel okay. This comparison thing leads to competition. Which kid reads first, runs fastest, is better at x or y. Does it matter?

Sometimes I can't even compare *me* to *me* from day to day. Some days I need more sleep, some days more food, some days more salt in my diet. Variability seems to rule my life within and between events.

Lenny wanted to learn how to be a nicer man so that his wife wouldn't leave him; he was just too slow of a learner. So was Carla. She spent twenty-three years waiting to see if Lenny would change. He changed, but it was as hard to see as the hair growing on his head.

Often, my students will watch me role-play or actually perform a therapy session with a real or mock client. Afterwards they will say how they wish they could do what I do as well as I do it. What an insult that is! If they could do what took me twenty years to learn, then what I do must not be too difficult. It took me a long time to learn to be a good therapist ... I couldn't learn it well until I was ready ... same as everything else.

At night, my children never go to sleep until they are ready, which is never as early as I want it to be. I never seem to want to wake up when the morning comes; my body awakes when it is ready.

We do things when we are ready, not usually before. Hugh Prather, the author of <u>Notes To Myself</u>, says that if the desire is to (<u>fill in the blank</u>) and you don't (<u>fill in the blank</u>) then the desire is not to blank. For years I had things I thought I wanted to do, but I never did them. Prather would say I didn't really want to do any of them. I may have wanted to talk about doing them, but not actually do them. We see this pattern often with things like smoking, exercising, dieting, writing, and getting out of a bad relationship. The reality it that we cannot do anything until we are ready.

Is there something you believe you really want to do? What is it? If you're not doing it, chances are, that for whatever reason, you are not ready. It's important here that you not beat yourself up for not doing *it*—that won't help. Instead, nurture yourself, care about yourself, and forgive yourself for not being able to do *it*. That way, you will have saved your energy, rather than using it to harm yourself, and you may then be more ready to do *it*.

Carla wanted to leave Lenny. Rachel wanted to learn her times tables. Joni wanted to quit smoking cigarettes. Joseph wanted to stop drinking. Betty wanted to exercise more. It seems that we all have something we want to be ready to do, but we don't do it, usually, because we're not ready.

What do you want to do? Figure that out, and then get ready. Some would argue that if you wait until you're "ready" to do something, you might never actually do it—whatever "it" is. My experience is actually the opposite—we do what we're ready to do when we're ready to do it—and not a moment before.

Carla got ready, it took a while, but she finally did it. Now Lenny's alone, and Carla is happy. What's it going to take for you to get ready?

8

Snipe Hunting

How do you find something you've never seen? There is something that most people look for just about every day. They come to therapy to learn about it yet they have never really seen it. It sounds next to impossible, doesn't it? It is. Most of us walk through this life looking for something we've rarely, if ever, seen: a truly great relationship.

Even as a child, I was a romantic. I wanted to find true love. Not love like I saw in my family or in my neighborhood—better love, perfect love, secure, loving love. I'm not sure what I was thinking, it's kind of silly really, to think that I could've looked for and found something I had never seen.

When we were kids there was this game that, at first, got *played* on us, and later, we *played* on others. It was called "snipe hunting." Did you ever play that? You only get it "played" on you once, unless you're really dumb. It goes like this: You get a bag and a flashlight and, when it gets dark, everyone goes out to try to bag a snipe. Everyone seems to be having so much fun, so of course, you go along. The only problem is that *you* are the game (perhaps, though I never thought of it this way, you are the snipe and you're being bagged just by playing). When you ask, "What does a snipe look like?" you are simply told *'you'll know when you see one.'*

Everyone laughs and runs off, looking for something they've never seen. There is no such thing as a snipe. You get it played on you just once, but you can play it on others as often as you find kids who have never heard of the game. Relationships are like that too, except I don't think anybody is laughing.

One of the topics I get to lecture about is relationships. Often, I will begin the class by asking that people show me, by raising their hands, how many of them want to be mathematicians, scientists, journalists or historians. I ask each question individually, and usually get a small number of hands for each question. Then I ask how many of them have had courses in each of these subjects, and every hand goes up. I follow this survey with another, asking how many of them plan to be "partnered or married" some day and almost every hand goes up. Then I ask, how many students have had a course or even a class on the subject, and few, if any hands go up. Then I ask, "What is wrong with this picture?"

The most painful question to have answered, though, is this: "With a show of fingers, how many truly great relationships have you seen? So great, that you would aspire to have one like it for yourself?" Sadly, the "mode" (or most common answer) is usually one or zero; the mean or average is usually two (some people actually put up four or five fingers leading to the mean of two when the mode is one or none!

How do we find something we've never or rarely seen? Has anyone ever caught a snipe? The sad reality is that about one in two marriages end. And, of the relationships that do not reach the point of a *formal* commitment, nearly 100% of them end; they end so that people can go on to look for their next possibility of a better relationship.

All over the United States there are people searching for something they have rarely seen, attempting to bag a snipe. But it isn't funny, it isn't a game, and nobody's laughing. Of the clients I see, approximately 80% of them come to work on the relationships they have or the ones they seek.

What is going on here? Why can't we find something we seem to want so badly? Are we *that* unlovable? I don't think so. I think we are afraid to risk, afraid to be hurt, afraid to give something that may not ever be given back in the same condition, like lending your car or a tool to a neighbor, but more fragile.

Who doesn't want to love or be loved? How can we find something we have hardly ever seen?

I guess we just keep looking until we find that snipe or we give up. Terry came to see me about this and shared how she wanted a man with whom to share her life more than anything else. I asked her to tell me how she spent her time in a "typical" week. She told me about her job, her schooling, her house and her immediate family. She mentioned nothing about her "work" in finding a significant relationship in life. We made a pie chart of how she spends her time and I showed her that she spends NO time trying to get a relationship. I asked her to list her priorities in life and she put marriage and kids in first place, with family, school, home, and work as 2nd, 3rd, 4th and 5th. With this illustration she saw that she had her stated priorities and her actual priorities as vastly different. She sat in my office dumbfounded at the simplicity of this lesson. She saw that she could never bag a snipe unless she took some time to look. Very few people have someone randomly knock on their door and express a desire to marry them. So, to bag a snipe one has to play—even if they don't have any idea about what a snipe might look like.

As with most challenges in life, you will pay a price for looking and you will pay a price for not looking; if you have not yet found what you are looking for, the choice today is yours.

Get your flashlight and your bag ready, but first, you might want to find out what a snipe looks like to you. Good luck.

9

The BIG Cover-Up

Jerry was the kind of man who knew everything about everything. The kind of man who knew so much that even when he *didn't* know something he would still convince you he knew things he didn't even know. You know the type. Jerry could *do* everything too. Sometimes, it was great having a man like Jerry around. If you needed a job done that nobody wanted to do, Jerry would do it just to show everybody he was the best at it. Whenever somebody needed volunteers for moving day, Jerry was there. He could fill the truck better than anyone else could, Jerry knew how to pack and load a truck better than anybody. Jerry was big AND strong. He could lift almost anything and he rarely needed help.

Jerry wondered why people didn't really like him. He wondered why he was never really close to anybody. Jerry couldn't understand this phenomenon; after all, he was always willing to lend a hand.

Jerry wasn't a bad looking man, and he didn't lack for ego. On the outside, Jerry looked like he had it all together. But on the inside, Jerry was scared, really scared.

When Jerry went on dates with women, he was always in charge; Jerry thought that this was what women wanted. He came to therapy to discuss his inability to make any real close friends, with men or women. He told me two stories of recent dates he'd had with women.

The first date was with a schoolteacher who had wanted his help putting up a bulletin board for her class—not *decorating* a bulletin board, actually putting it up. She thought that would be fun, and Jerry was good at everything, so he thought this would be a great opportunity to have a date and to show his stuff. On the date, Jerry took his hammer, nails, drill, screws and his level; this was to be a functional *and* fun date.

He told me he'd wanted to show his date how to use the drill to put up the bulletin board. According to Jerry, she was really lousy at drilling. He said he even got a little mad at how poorly she had done. Jerry liked to do things right. His father, who was a lot like Jerry, always taught him that if he were going to do a job, he should do it right. Unfortunately, Jerry had learned his lesson too well. That evening, Jerry was so busy putting the bulletin board up right that he forgot to notice his date wasn't really having much fun.

When the night was over, the bulletin board looked great. Jerry had done an excellent job with installation, of course. Jerry could *do* practically everything. Jerry thought that the date went well and couldn't understand why the schoolteacher never wanted to see him again.

Jerry's other dating story ended the same way and concluded with a similar outcome. This time, Jerry's date wanted to go fishing. Jerry thought he had found the perfect woman, a woman who wanted to fish. Naturally, he was great at fishing. So on this date, my client set out to teach this woman how to bait a hook. He tried and he tried, but she just couldn't seem to get it right. Jerry got frustrated, baited her hook for her, and they caught a lot of fish. To Jerry, this was a very good day fishing. But in the end, this woman never returned

Jerry's calls after this date, and Jerry didn't know why. After all, the date had gone so well, Jerry told me that they "caught a ton of fish!"

Jerry didn't get it. He couldn't figure out why people didn't want to be with him. Oh sure, sometimes his friends told him that he made people uncomfortable, especially women, but he just didn't believe it. Jerry also insisted that he was *nothing* like his father … he said his father was, "a real bastard, who meant well." Growing up, Jerry had thought he could never do anything right—at least, never do anything good enough for his father. He said he'd wanted to do everything well because he didn't want to make his father mad. Even though his father died when Jerry was eighteen, Jerry was still trying to please him.

Occasionally, Jerry impressed me with his insight into understanding himself. In one session he almost cried and said, "Damn, I do to people the same thing my old man did to me." Jerry wanted to be a good client; after all, Jerry was good at everything.

Can you see what is wrong with Jerry? Jerry has his emotions all flipped up. Jerry is not unusual for a man; he's like a lot of men. He shows anger and frustration as a cover for how sad and afraid he is. Jerry is afraid, he's very afraid, and, like many men, he was taught as a boy to **never** show this fear to anyone. He was taught that to show his fear would make him vulnerable, and then others could get the upper hand and take advantage of him. Jerry learned this lesson very well. Perhaps he learned it too well.

Because of his fear, Jerry is "road rage" waiting to happen. When asked what he is like when he drives, Jerry said, "People are assholes. Nobody knows how to drive." He then proceeded to tell me a story about some idiot who'd cut him off, without a turn signal, and almost sent him into a pole just before he got to my office. He told me he was so mad he felt like killing someone.

While it certainly appeared that Jerry was mad it wasn't really anger. Jerry's anger was a cover-up for his fear. Men get angry when they are scared, because they're not *allowed* to be scared or sad. Men learn early on if they cry merely for fear or sadness, their fathers or coaches will "really" give them something to cry about. So men get tough and bury their sadness and their fear.

Jerry was taught that doing something right was more important than being connected to the people with whom he was working or playing. Baiting the hook, hanging the bulletin board—these two things were much more important than making certain his female companions were enjoying themselves. Didn't they *want* to do it right?

Jerry needed to learn the difference between 'the process' and 'the outcome.' This was a difficult lesson to teach, but it was a much more important lesson for Jerry than how to fix, build and pack things well. For Jerry, this lesson was life or death. Can you see why Jerry is scared? Jerry will live and die alone if he doesn't learn this lesson. Can you see why Jerry is sad?

Do you know Jerry? I know lots of Jerrys, I don't really like them very much, they scare me, but you'd never know it, because all you ever see me get is mad. I learned my lessons well too. The lessons we learn as children surrounded by other boys don't help us when we try to find women to share our lives with when we are men. No wonder we're so sad and scared. After a lifetime of knowing or pretending how to do everything, we just don't know what to do.

Jerry is in a ton of pain and he knows it. But you'll never hear that from him, he wasn't allowed to tell you or to show you, even if you asked. This is a very difficult client in therapy—they have to be convinced that therapy can help them—which is hard to do when they've always thought that psychology was bull. The work is to tap into their pain and give them hope. Hope that they can learn to do things differently, and they can. Jerry is a motivated client, ready, willing and able to learn—and with the right counselor, this man will do the work by being challenged to change, just like his football coach was able to challenge him to learn the plays. Jerry does well with behaviors, he's a good student once he gets ready to get in touch with and rid of the pain. Be direct with Jerry, get him to a tough therapist and watch him get as good at relationships as he is with bulletin boards.

10

Like Father, Like Son

Steve was usually a happy man. He often came in to talk about his new career and how excited he was that he had changed jobs in his 30s. He spoke often about his marriage and how lucky he was to have such a wonderful woman sharing his life. He celebrated how well things were going in his life and he discussed how he simply wanted to fine-tune those aspects of his life that needed minor adjustments. But today was different. I could see it as soon as Steve sat down.

Steve was sad today but his mind and thoughts were clear. In many ways life was not turning out the way Steve had predicted it would. The luster was off, the shine was gone and Steve found himself stuck dead center in the Land of Reality. Steve was seeing, just as he had feared, that the sun didn't always shine here. Worse than that, he was beginning to see he had become his father, and his father's father, and his father's father's father.

Steve never wanted to be "just like his father." It's not that his father was bad in any way. It was just that Steve wanted to take the lessons his father had taught him and do life better. Steve's father—like my father and maybe your father—lived a life that was sadly routine. You know the pattern: Get up, drink coffee, go to work, come home, read the paper, eat dinner, watch TV, go to bed, and then get up and do it again.

Steve was afraid to look in the mirror, because it wasn't just one mirror he was looking into, it was mirrors reflecting other mirrors. You may have seen this phenomenon when mirrors reflect other mirrors, you can see how they appear to turn in their own reflection. This is what Steve saw as he examined his life. He saw the image of his life somehow turning awkwardly with the reflection of itself; it was clear that the ancestral lines of Steve's family went on forever, and appeared to be continuing on through yet another generation, much to Steve's dismay.

Steve didn't want to live a routine, boring, robotic life. He set out early in life not to "work in a factory" like his father. Steve couldn't understand how he had never really seen the similarities before. He worked hard to change his career every time he grew bored, finding routine patterns as the order of the day. He went to college when he was 18 and then returned for graduate school to ensure he would not find routine in his life like his father and his father's father had. Unfortunately, the reality was that Steve had become a "factory worker" just like his father, in spite of himself.

No, Steve's life, mine too, were going to be different. We were going to be better than *routine*, we were not going to wake up, go to work, come home, go to sleep, only to wake up to do it again, amen. We were not going to allow that to happen. Our work lives were going to have meaning and not be boring. And yet, in spite of our efforts, we were starting to feel stuck, just like our father.

I recall a conversation with my grandfather when I was nine or so, when he asked me what I wanted to be when I grew up. I'd told him I wasn't sure but I wanted to do something I enjoyed; I told him I wanted to be happy. I remember how he laughed at me and said, *"Happy! What's happy? Men don't enjoy their work. Work is work; it's not to be enjoyed. Nobody enjoys work—that's what makes it work!"* I'll never forget him laughing at me. I'll bet Steve's grandfather was laughing too.

I think this is why Steve was sad when he came to see me. He was sad because he was finding out that despite his lifelong attempts to have a better life than his father, he was actually living the same life. Oh, it was better, but it was also the same. The same in so many ways that it pained him to look at it.

But this was therapy, and looking at his life is what he was here to do.

Why hadn't he seen this happening along the way? He had worked so hard to make sure this would never happen to him. The answer is clear. Most animals work to avoid pain in life. Men are especially good at staying away from the pain they are experiencing, both physical and emotional. When babies place their hand on something hot, they will automatically withdraw their hand in an effort to avoid pain. Being out of pain is a universal human drive. Steve was only following the pattern of the human experience by not feeling the pain he was in. Fortunately, or unfortunately, Steve came to therapy after he noticed the burn mark on his hand.

What can men (or women, for that matter) do? Are we destined to continue to live our lives like our parents, following pattern after pattern? What is it that makes the legacy of family histories continue? How often do you see single parents give birth to children who become single parents? How usual is it for parents who cheat on their spouses to have children who cheat on their spouses? What makes an abused child turn into an abusive parent, only to give birth to another abused child who becomes another abusive parent? How is it that factory workers become the parents of other factory workers?

Steve came to therapy to find out. He walked through the doors of *my* factory, and together we began to examine life by looking in the mirror. You know what we saw? We saw our fathers and grandfathers ... and I heard my grandfather asking, "Happy? What's happy?" And then I heard myself asking Steve the very same question.

So we struggled, together, in therapy to come up with an answer to a question that my grandfather had asked so many years ago. What IS happy and how can a person find this elusive, changeable thing? Perhaps Steve will use his therapy to challenge himself to find his answer by walking toward his pain and looking in his mirror—unfortunately, I'm not really sure if there's any other way.

11

When Help Isn't Help

When Phyllis was 20 she had her first child, a son. Two years later, she had her second child, a daughter. The oldest, David, was a "high maintenance" baby. He cried a lot and demanded constant attention. Phyllis wanted to be a good mom, so she gave David everything he needed. Her daughter, Amy, was more independent from the time she was born. (Phyllis never believed that genetics had much to do with how people acted until she had children of her own to observe.) Phyllis never married, and David and Amy's father didn't want much to do with his children, or with Phyllis, so Phyllis was on her own.

Phyllis tried very hard to meet David's needs, which were many. Phyllis wondered why David was like this, especially when Amy was so easy. Phyllis thought that if she could just keep meeting David's needs then someday he would feel nourished and full and he would then be able to meet his own needs. Phyllis was wrong about this.

When Phyllis came to talk in therapy her main goal was to figure out "what she had done so wrong" in raising David. People often want to know what they have done wrong, as if understanding it would somehow turn back the clock and change things; it doesn't.

My patients seem to think gaining insight into who and how they are (or were) will somehow make things different. Somehow, the concept of *insight* got a lot of credit in the field of psychotherapy because almost everyone who comes in wants to have more of it than they already have.

The classic story is about Little Albert, who came in to find out why he was afraid of white furry things; he spent years in therapy to find out why, but when he found out why, he was *still* afraid of white furry things. Apparently, insight wasn't enough for Little Albert.

Phyllis knew she had done everything she could for David, and much less for Amy, and yet Amy grew up to be a hard worker, a good friend, a college graduate, a wife and a mother. Phyllis couldn't see how this happened. David got older and frankly, never grew up. He cheated in school, got in trouble frequently, had few friends, and the friends he had were as delinquent as he was. David was in prison by the time Phyllis came to see me.

Can you see what happened here? It's a sad, but not an unusual story. It confused Phyllis so much that she sought help to understand something that could not be undone. She began her therapy crying and saying that she knew parents aren't suppose to have favorites, but she had always favored David. She thought he was special from the day he was born. He *needed* her—no one else ever really did. Amy was special too, but she didn't need a mother the same way her son did. Phyllis cried, said she had just done what she thought was right, and lamented, "How could David do this me?"

She *had* done her best, she did what she thought was right. She met the needs of her son, and she had done a great job, perhaps too great. She had done her job so well that David never learned he could do some things on his own. Amy learned early in life that mom wasn't going to be there to do everything for her; after all, she was busy with David. If Amy needed something done, she would often have to do it for herself. Mom had "trained" both David and Amy to be like they were. I told Phyllis that people are just animals that get conditioned, a lot like Pavlov's dogs.

David and Amy learned their lessons well. David learned that he could always find someone to take care of things for him, and today he has a warm place to sleep and three (not very good) meals a day. They do take care of you in prison.

Janet was another mother who came to therapy to tell me about her son. She didn't mention how old he was when the session began; she simply told me she was doing a lot for him, to help him out, and wanted to know how to better help him. She told me that her son had borrowed a lot of money—some of it to begin his own business (that went bad). She'd even given him her car, and now she had little money and no car. She said that her son would never do anything for her or for other family members. Janet deduced that her son needed *more* help than she was giving him and she wanted to know what she could do to help him more.

She finally told me her son was 35. I told her about Phyllis.

In psychology we often tell people that the definition of insanity is doing the same thing over and over again and expecting different results. We say, if you keep doing what you're doing, you're going to keep getting what you're getting. We are, indeed, just animals.

Phyllis and Janet were very loving mothers. They did what they thought they should do to raise their children. And now, it was time to change what they were doing. Often in therapy with very caring and loving parents, I have to explain the concept that sometimes, helping isn't really helping. Life is full of paradox and this is one of them.

Giving to another is a very nice thing, until the giving isn't really giving, it's actually *taking*. It's hard to see this while it's happening; Phyllis never did. Her daughter saw it, even as a young child she would tell her mother to let David do things on his own, but Phyllis loved David too much. She never learned that there was another way to love him.

One story I like to tell my clients is that when I began working as a therapist I was six foot four inches tall. I wanted to help so much that I would pick people up and take them home with me. Since my hands were full I would carry them on my shoulders. One day, I noticed I was no longer six foot four. I was only six feet tall. That was fine with me. There were a lot of people who needed my help so, I took more people home, on my shoulders of course, and my hands were full. I dropped to five foot eight and continued to take people on, until one day I noticed I was only five foot four, and I threw everyone off my shoulders screaming, "Five foot four is as short as any adult man should have to be in the United States! Get off of me!"

I learned that my helping wasn't helping. It wasn't helping me and it wasn't helping others. The ironies here are many. Perhaps most salient to me was the fact that the people I took home weren't getting better, and the *helping* behaviors that Janet, Phyllis and I had developed out of love turned us into angry, bitter people.

Ironically, David hated his mother, so did Janet's son. Ironically, Janet and Phyllis began to hate their sons. I began resenting the people I was helping—they weren't getting better and they actually came to expect more!

This "helping thing" is obviously very confusing … the answers are not very easy to find. The lesson here for me is that I liked being six feet tall a lot better than I like being five feet tall. I learned that sometimes what I think I'm doing to help people is actually not very helpful at all. I learned that sometimes, the most help I can give someone is to allow him or her to figure some things out on his or her own. It may be too late for Phyllis and Janet's sons to understand this lesson, but it might not be too late for Phyllis, Janet, you or me.

12

Dancing at the Center of the Universe

"Well, it's a marvelous night for a moon dance with the stars up above in your eyes, a fantabulous night to make romance 'neath the cover of October skies ..."

Van Morrison, a white man with soul, sings this song—it has always has been one of my favorites.

Two weeks ago the moon was full, the sky was clear, the temperature was in the 60s. I placed my headphones on, set the volume and listened to a variety of different songs by various artists. Tryst, my Golden Retriever, and I set off for the field near our house.

The air was crisp and clear; I could feel the night air on my face as I walked along the trail between the grass and weeds that had grown up to my knees. There were crickets cricketing as my feet crunched the grass beneath me. There was a quiet in the air that only nighttime can seem to bring, almost like a hush in the air. As I walked a Kenny Loggins song came on and I started to skip a little, moving to the music. As I turned around I saw my moon shadow turning to face me. All self-consciousness went away and I began to dance. The field was calm and dark, I was away from the houses in the suburb and my

43

body began to move, to dance, a moon dance, alone. Tryst ran through the field as she always does, and I let go of all inhibitions and continued to dance. I must've looked like a madman!

I hadn't felt this liberated since I first fell in love with this song. Van the Man was absolutely right; I hadn't felt this free and unabashed since my childhood when acting crazy was acceptable. Van was right it was indeed, marvelous.

I was so free and unencumbered. The music blared in my headphones for only me to hear and I let go, dancing a moon dance with my moon shadow. I found myself lost in the world, lost in the universe, lost in space and time, dancing to music only I could hear, with a person only I could see: me. Dancing with the moon and me. I was *this-close* to crazy, and it was perfect.

My head was spinning in a clearer way than it had before my walk began—perhaps this is what happens on the edge of crazy—and I became aware of a number of things. I became aware that in every moment I live, I am as *young* as I'll ever be, and at the very same time, I am as *old* as I've ever been. Both of those events are occurring at exactly the same time every moment I am alive.

As I looked up into the sky following my moon dance, I was also aware, as I often am when gazing at the immensity of the universe, that if the sky goes on forever (and surely it must) then I am—at all times—dead-set in the middle of the universe, and so is everyone else.

Dancing at the center of the universe, a moon dance, dancing with me, both old and young all at the same time, dancing. A lucid moment of insanity, just for me.

I had never been this crazy before; it was fairly unusual for me to be *this* crazy. But it was okay. I was comfortable with my craziness, so was Tryst, and the moon didn't seem to mind either.

13

It's MY Opinion!

Reader's Digest has to be one of the most amazing publications of all time. I don't know if there is anyone who hasn't heard of it or read it at some time in his or her life. The size, feel and sight of that magazine takes me back to places and times in my childhood like no other written material can.

One day a few months ago, I was reading an issue of Reader's Digest and came across the quote, *"If two people agree on everything, there's no need for one of them."* Wow! How profound I thought this statement to be. I began to think about conflict and how all conflict relates to the concept of disagreeing and how it is that if we agree on everything then there's no need for the other person.

In my work with couples in marriage and couples therapy, and in my presentations on relationships, I have often mused that the "strength" of all relationships is conflict and the ability to deal with and work through it. Hell, anyone can enjoy and appreciate the things about another with which they like and agree; but your ability to care about, love and nurture that which you dislike or disagree with leads to lasting, intimate, and loving relationships.

Why then, do we have so much difficulty with difference and disagreements? If two people agree on everything, there is no need for one of them, right? Of course that's right. For example, have you ever gone out to eat with someone, perhaps a first or second date, or with a new friend, and you are looking at the menu when your friend says, "Hey, you should try their lasagna, they have the greatest lasagna," and you say, "Hmmm, you know, I really don't like lasagna."

Then, your friend looks at you all offended, as if she or he was the one who gave the families' grandmother's recipe to the cook. Don't try this on the first date if you want the relationship to go anywhere. Explore this kind of disagreement with movies too. Did you ever come out of a movie in which your friend *loved* the movie and you were lukewarm on it, and your friend says, "*Wow, that was great wasn't it? I am so psyched, I can't wait to see it again!*" And you're thinking, "*Jeez, I don't think I got it … I didn't like that at all.*" But you dare not say that; after all, your friend *loved* the movie, so in order to keep peace you (essentially lie and) say, "Yeah, I thought it was pretty good too." You dare not say what you really think, especially if you *hated* it. You don't want to offend this other person. Even though they actually had nothing more to do with the movie than pay to see it.

What is this about? Why is it so hard to disagree, to be totally honest?

I was doing therapy with a couple just last week—very intelligent, highly educated people. I asked them what brought them to therapy, and they told me it was premarital counseling. The two had a relatively new relationship. They were both in their mid-thirties and had been in numerous failed relationships. They were determined not to make the same mistakes again. During the course of the therapy hour, the woman said she thought that sometimes he stayed over at her house when he really didn't want to, because he was afraid that if he went home it would hurt her and push her "abandonment issues." Without hesitation, the man agreed that he had indeed done this.

At this point I interrupted and asked her if she knew what she was doing by saying this. She said no ... so, I told her. I looked at him and said, "With all due respect ..." (that is actually a great line to start with when you are going to say something pretty critical), "she is calling you a liar! She is saying that sometimes you lie to her in order to keep her from getting mad or sad. Essentially, you are lying to keep the peace!" Isn't that ironic and foolish to lie to *help* the relationship? Well, long term, it won't work. Why did he do this? Because he was afraid that his opinion would cause more harm than good.

Here's another example. I was talking to my father and my stepmother over lunch one day and the topic of TV shows came up. My father and stepmother actually had the audacity to say that they didn't like *Seinfeld*. They said they didn't quite get what all the excitement was about this show, and it was no big deal to them that it was going off the air. Imagine that! They didn't like George, Elaine, Jerry and Kramer! In my foolishness, I felt offended, as if I were either some close friend of Jerry's or one of the show's writers. When, in actuality, all I ever had to do with the show was turn on the TV and watch it. So, I argued with them about why they **should** like *Seinfeld* ... silly me, I had forgotten the lesson I worked so hard to teach.

This discussion led to some underlying tension that had existed in my relationship with my father and stepmother (this was the blessing in disguise I guess), and my stepmother said, "You know Mark, you always think your opinion and way of doing things is better than everybody else's!"

At this, I laughed ... which is never a good thing to do during an emotionally charged argument ... I laughed and said, "Of course I do! Of course I think my opinion is better than anybody else's, **that's what makes it MY opinion!**" I went on to say, "If I liked your opinion better, then that would become my opinion." That's what opinions are—each of our choices about what to think, believe, feel, do, eat, and enjoy. Why does my opinion have to be offensive to your opinion?

It doesn't. What we have to do is learn how to share different opinions more effectively, more honestly, less offensively. After awhile we will decide if we have enough common opinions to share a relationship. If we have too many views that are contrary to each other we will probably choose not to be together much. But you don't have to be offended if I don't like the food you like or the movies or TV programs you choose. Actually, if I can relax my insecurities and defenses I can probably learn from the differences in opinion you bring to the table. Hell, if everyone agrees with everything, there'll be no need for any of us!

My goal for today is to allow myself to accept disagreements with others openly. I will work to allow myself to recognize when I am less than honest in my decisions so as not to offend. I will try to be more truthful, believing that not telling the truth—just to keep the peace—is an irony I don't want to live with.

14

I Get a Kick Out of You

Lori returned to therapy after a three year absence asking the very same question she had asked the last time she was in: "How can I make it stop?"

She told me she had worked **so** hard to end the dysfunctional relationship with Tom, she was **certain** she could end it eventually. Lori wanted to find some peace in the torture. She *knew* she loved Tom and she knew that he was **no good** for her (everyone in her life couldn't be wrong), but she **just** couldn't end it, even though she knew she had to.

Lori had tried everything to be done with Tom, a man she had been dating on and off since high school. Nothing seemed to work. Tom was in Lori like Kool-Aid in water; no matter what she did, she couldn't get the Kool-Aid out of the water. All she could hope to do was dilute the water. She attempted to dilute the water with tears, hoping that if she could feel enough pain, she could wash him out of her life forever. For Lori, it was over, but it was never done. She wanted it over and done, and this just never seemed to happen no matter how much time passed between contacts. Tom was in Lori and Lori wanted him out.

This is not an uncommon story, it happens to a lot of people. Women are not the only ones stuck in this pattern, it happens to men too. Everyone asks the same question: "How can you get to the end, resolve the pain and move on?"

There are no simple answers to this question. Many people have literally wasted their entire lives waiting for the relationship to change, to improve, and to become what they had dreamt it could be. After investing huge amounts of time in the relationship, people are often more likely to stay, in an attempt to justify the time they have already put in. There appears to be no way out. No justification for staying in the relationship, no justification for ending it. If they stay, they look stupid, if they leave, they feel stupid. Catch-22.

"The worse part," Lori said, "is that no one seems to understand. Everyone just thinks I'm stupid. People act as if I could just end it, no problem. Why can't they understand? I don't even have anyone left to talk to about this. I've lost all my closest friends."

Lori was all alone. So were Helen, David, Chris and Joe. There are times as a therapist when half my caseload is made up of people like Lori—people stuck in relationships that are slowly draining the life out of them, a virtual club of people in relationships that are over, but never done. People wounded by the drama of falling in love with someone who is so addicting that getting off cigarettes or heroin would seem to be easier. People reinforced by the intermittent schedule of reward that looks a lot like love and affection, and causes them to return, repeatedly, to the source of their pain and pleasure.

Lori wanted me to help her understand how she could go from being a secure, confident, attractive person to someone she couldn't even recognize. She also wanted me to figure out Tom so that she could understand him and his motivation in ruining her life. People often want help figuring out people in their lives. They pay good money to do what I call "ghost therapy," the therapy that attempts to understand the others in their life. (Ghost therapy is impossible to do and I refuse to do it. I can barely help the people who are in my office, I sure can't help the ones who aren't!)

Someday, I think scientists will broaden their list of addictive substances to include qualities or chemicals found in certain types of people. This is not unlike the fact that if one parent is an alcoholic there is a greater chance that they will have a child who is also addicted than the non-addicted parent who has a child. I think someday they will find this true of certain people with certain other people. Lori was—and is—addicted to Tom. He is no better for her than alcohol is to an alcoholic. It's not her fault, but it *is* her responsibility to do something about it.

Have you not felt a chemical charge or pull toward (and also away from) certain people? Tom has something that Lori is addicted to. It's biological. The only thing she could've done is never to have met Tom. The fact that Lori sees her attraction to Tom as "her fault," that she has "blamed" herself for ruining her life, is of no help to her in ending the addiction. Actually, it's part of the problem. As she blames herself, she finds that she must punish herself for being so stupid. This blame, combined with the intermittent reinforcement, combined with the chemical pull toward him, has been a combination that has led to nine years of torture.

Lori is looking for peace in the torture, and she is finding none. If Lori is to move on she must begin with forgiving herself, getting away from Tom, avoiding all contact, and continuing to dilute the Kool-Aid with the tears she drops over the pain she is in.

In therapy, we often debate whether the client should change their attitudes first in the hope that behavioral change will follow, or if one should change behaviors in the hopes that attitudes or feelings will change. In the case of any kind of addiction, especially one to another person—the answer here is clear. GET AWAY! End all contact completely. No emails, no texts, no phone calls, no pictures, no visits to that coffee shop you used to go to, no contact with his (or her) friends, no questions about how she or he is doing. End all contact and in six to twelve months, the feelings will be different. But Lori better get started soon—it's already been nine years! If you're like Lori, I encourage you to try this method. Oh, and one more bit of therapeutic advice: If the end of the relationship is imminent and inevitable—ALWAYS be the one to end it. Good luck.

15

The Twilight Zone

Rod Serling must have been the coolest dude of all time. This man knew and saw things that the rest of us couldn't think of on our own if our lives depended on it. I learned so many lessons from "The Twilight Zone" when I was young. I learned about life, death, and the relativity of time; my mind races as I think to share just one of the lessons he taught me. He taught me so much, some intentional lessons, some lessons not so intentional. (I'll bet he never meant to teach me that smoking cigarettes would kill you, but he taught me that too. Sometime shortly after the start of the show, he would stand there, looking cool as hell, talking in that incredible voice of his, with his cigarette in hand, killing himself right in front of me. I think I was nine.)

One of my favorite episodes was the one where a 1950s type hoodlum gets killed somehow and after his death he meets Sebastian Cabot, Mr. French from the 1960s television show "Family Affair." If you don't who know he is, just picture a formally dressed, butler-looking man with impeccable manners and style. Well, Mr. French meets the hoodlum immediately upon his death and asks him what he wants. He tells the gangster dude he can have anything he'd like and it will be. So, of course the requests are obvious: money, beautiful women, and cars.

The gangster gets to go wherever he wants and do whatever he wants. He is rich in every way. In his giant mansion we see a pool table with women hanging on his every need, serving him joyfully. He shoots the cue ball and every shot goes in, to the laughing glee of the women who surround him. He decides to take off with the women and go to the track, and of course, every horse he picks is a winner. He simply cannot lose; he has everything he ever wanted in life. Twenty-three minutes and one commercial break later, gangster dude is getting sick of it. Winning every time is getting old. He has more money, women, cars and things than he ever dreamt of and he can't stand it. In the final scene (before Rod returns) he freaks out and runs to Mr. French screaming, *"What the hell is this, I didn't think heaven would be like this, I hate this!"*

At that, we see Mr. French, leaning back, chuckling to himself, tapping his rotund belly and saying, "Who said this was heaven?" The end.

Oh that Rod was a slick one. He wanted me to learn something here, what was it?

As an adult I got to take my kids to Disneyland. As I look back on my life as a father there are certain days that stand out as being absolutely perfect. Our day in Disneyland was one of them. The kids were good, the weather was clear, the lines weren't long, and the grounds were as clean as could possibly be. Every single moment of that day was perfect. I never wanted that day to end. Parenting in the real world was nothing like that; why couldn't every day be like that?

Driving home that night, exhausted, I remembered this episode of the Twilight Zone. I could never get the laughter of Mr. French out of my head ... and I heard him while I was driving home, the kids sound asleep in the backseat. It was clear that what made this day so great was that it *wasn't* normal, normal days aren't perfect. There's dirt and mess, clouds and rain. There's crying and fighting, sadness and pain.

And, that's good. For without the rain, how would we ever get to appreciate the sun? Living in Disneyland isn't all it's cracked up to be. I guess it's a nice place to visit, but I really don't think I want to live there.

16

What's the Difference?

John was a handsome man, strong jaw line, straight blonde hair, and the combination of soft and rugged good looks I'd always hoped to see in the mirror. He was a kind man with an underlying anger that was more apparent to others than it was to him. John was in such denial about his anger that he wondered why others weren't initially open to him. John figured people just didn't like him for reasons unknown.

Sharon too was a friendly enough woman. She was soft spoken with dark skin; she was pretty in a pleasant kind of way, not beautiful. Sharon was angry too, but her anger came out as sadness. Sometimes, in sessions, she would struggle to find words and she would get teary just sitting in therapy reflecting on her life. It's often like that with men and women; men who are sad look angry, woman who are angry look sad. That's what's socially acceptable. They came to me ten years and 1,800 miles apart, for different reasons and by way of different courses. But they felt similar things, for different reasons.

Both sets of parents—John's and Sharon's—constantly assured them that they were *"no different than anyone else."* Their parents meant well. I am certain all parents who say this phrase to their children mean well. But John had Cerebral Palsy, which caused his legs to contort into an awkward gait that twisted his body down to the left, then up as his crooked legs moved, one in front of the other. John's awkward gait was impossible to miss, clearly different from everyone else's. Everyone could see it—except John. John's walk was as normal to him as your walk is to you, and my walk is to me.

Sharon is Native American. Her biological ancestry is somewhat of a mystery, possibly Alaskan Native, but at any rate, her biological history is not Caucasian. A White family adopted Sharon shortly after she was born. Both Sharon and John's families had meant well when they told them they weren't any different than anybody else. They simply wanted their children to believe they could succeed just like the other kids. After all, it's the American way: the idea that we can all succeed if we just try hard enough is a lesson I received often. The lesson was that if I just tried harder, I'd be successful. If people simply pulled themselves up by their bootstraps, they'd get what they sought in life. This lesson is taught over and over again in the United States. It's a good lesson, but discounts the reality that some people may have been given better bootstraps to pull or better arms to pull them with. None of us want our kids thinking they can't make it; as parents we are taught to teach our kids they can succeed, no matter what! Many people still believe that one of the best ways to inspire our kids (especially children with some sort of "difference" or disability) is to tell them they are *just like everyone else*. The better message would be: "You are just as *good* as anyone else." It isn't really true that we all have the same chance at everything—and suggesting that we do can be a harmful lesson for some.

John went on to tell me many stories about his life throughout the course of his therapy. We worked to deal with helping him learn to connect with others in a way that felt more accepting, comfortable and intimate. I often found myself wanting to help John find ways to unleash his anger, provide a safe place for him to vent it, understand it and release it. Perhaps this would help John stop turning people off with the "edge" that other people saw, but John couldn't see. Perhaps this anger was another thing that made John different.

One day, John told me about a class trip he took in sixth grade, when he was twelve years old. The class visited a large city in the downtown area. They were walking in a straight line, as elementary school kids often do during field trips. John was toward the back of the line, looking straight ahead as his class walked toward a high-rise building made of reflective glass. While John studied the reflection made by this long line of twenty-five classmates, he noticed one kid toward the back who leaned and moved up and down, forward, back, and to the left as he walked. John watched this strange sight as he approached the building, confused and curious, wondering who the odd kid was—he'd never seen him before.

When John reached the part of the building where his section of the line passed the mirrored window he gasped. He hoped that no one had heard him; he didn't want to bring any more attention to himself. He bit his lip, wincing as he held back tears. What John had just realized was that HE was the kid with the incredibly unusual walk. John continued to watch his body move, as he had never seen it before, and for the first time, things began to make sense to him. He *wasn't* like everyone else; he was different, very different. No wonder he couldn't shoot a basketball like his friends, no wonder he couldn't run as fast or play baseball as well. John's parents had meant well, but they forgot to tell him that he *was* different, in a profound way. Of course John was different—we all are. Some of us are just different in ways that are easier to notice than others.

Sharon too was told she was no different than anyone else. Sharon could never understand why the other children treated her as if she were. She heard over and over from her parents that she was just like everyone else. *She* heard it—the other kids didn't. She too realized one day, much later in life than John, that she *was* (and is) different—and—right or wrong—people treated her differently because of her difference. Even her parents had treated her differently; they'd never told her Anglo brother that he "was no different than the other kids." Sharon and John were so different that they had to be reminded that they were no different. If you have to be told you're just like everyone else, that probably means you're really not.

John and Sharon are different than everyone else—they always were. You are different too, so am I. The challenge for us in this lesson is to realize that our differences don't have to handicap us; we are all challenged in some way, some ways more visible than others. In their therapy, John and Sharon were forced to look at themselves more honestly. They were forced to see things they had never seen. I have to do this too—so do you. It's important that each of us take a good, hard look inside ourselves to examine our differences. Acknowledge them, accept them, explore them and learn from them. John and Sharon were hiding from the things that made them different, and this led to anger, frustration and confusion. By acknowledging the aspects of who we are and exploring (rather than denying) what makes each of us different, we are more able to release the confusion that may lead to our anger and embrace that which makes us unique.

Each of us must realistically explore the blessings and handicaps we have and make this day one in which we see ourselves more clearly with our own two eyes. When we are able to do this we not only are more able to connect with others, we are more able to accept and connect with ourselves.

It took some time and some pushing, but John and Sharon finally do.

17

Out of Control

It was almost 10:00 p.m. on a Tuesday night when I sat down to attempt to write some of this book. The younger kids were up later than usual because of a school-sponsored skating party earlier in the evening. My 9-year-old and 11-year-old fell fast asleep, but the 4-year-old was wired to the max. She didn't want to go to sleep; in fact, it seemed like she *couldn't* go to sleep. So, she did what most any tenacious pre-school child would do when *forced* against her will: She cried. No, more than that, she threw a fit.

Typing and thinking had become impossible; the distraction was overwhelming. I tried to keep typing, I wanted to write, but I was overcome by *feeling*. My feelings spun out of control. My hands were shaking, my heart was racing and I was feeling very frustrated and angry. I could almost feel my blood boiling. I *felt* like doing unspeakable things to my child. (I had never really understood acts of immediate, out-of-control child abuse until I had kids. Most people with children know this feeling, but rarely admit it. It's downright scary.)

Earlier that day, a client named Sarah came to therapy complaining that she found some condoms in her boyfriend's travel bag. She was so angry she didn't know what to do. Her hands were shaking, her heart was racing and she was feeling frustrated and angry. She left her house for work feeling overwhelmed with grief and anger. After our session, she went home; it was four hours later and she found that she was in a much better mood to talk. Sarah and I both knew that there must be a lesson in here somewhere.

Human beings have essentially three ways of functioning in the world: We have our cognitions, or our thinking; we have our behaviors, or our actions; and, we have our affect, or our feelings. Of these three ways of being, we can (mostly) control two of the three. Usually, we can control *what we do*; and to a lesser extent, we can control *what we think*. But rarely (at least, most difficult) can we control *what we feel*.

When Beth was crying the other night, I wanted to control my feelings. I wanted to stop feeling so bugged. I wanted to relax, calm down, and just type. But I couldn't. I talked to myself a lot. Psychologists call this "cognitive restructuring."

I said all the right things. Almost out loud, I said, *"She's over-tired, she's just a baby, she can't control herself, she'll be asleep soon, relax Mark, it's okay, shut-up Beth, SHUT-UP BETH, DAMN IT! CAN'T SOMEBODY SHUT HER UP!?"* It was awful. I thought I should leave the house, walk the dog, come back to writing in a few minutes, and this is what I did. An hour later, I didn't feel the same anger or frustration as I felt when I left the house. In this moment, I realized that I had control over my thinking and what I could do (my actions), but I did not have control over my feelings—at least, not as long as I was sitting there listening to her fit.

Sarah and I were having the same struggle. When she found the condoms in Martin's travel bag, following a trip he had just taken to Chicago, she was livid, sad, confused and scared. She *wanted* to control her feelings, she didn't want to *feel* these things, but she did. She, too, tried to talk herself out of the feelings she was having but it was impossible. She could control what she did, and to a lesser extent, what she thought, but she could not control how she felt.

Some people are more ruled by their heads (their thoughts), some by their actions. But most, it seems, are driven by emotion, which can be both a blessing and a curse.

The more I witness and study human behavior in others (and in myself) the more I see that our emotions can be the most honest, dangerous and wonderful parts of who we are. Our emotions are so incredibly truthful that our control *over* them is difficult, at least initially, until we take some action behaviorally and cognitively. For me, emotion always seems to trump cognition and behavior—therefore often seeming to control both.

On the night that I was trying to type and Beth was "making" me crazy, I knew that I could have left the room or the house. I could have altered my thoughts, which I tried to do, but my affect quickly led me back to my anger. I could not change that her behavior was making me crazy. In my early days of studying psychology a popular lesson was being taught—you probably heard it—which said, "Nobody can *make* you *feel* anything." Remember that? They said, you got to choose how you felt about any given situation. I don't believe that. People and situations often "make us" feel certain ways, and I can certainly "make" someone feel good or bad (bad is easier) about himself or herself.

Clearly, each of us must examine which aspect of our being is more in charge. Take a good look at yourself today. Which aspect of you is driving your life? Is it your thinking, your feeling or your behaviors? What do you lead with? My friend Dominic Brewer leads with his thinking. He is pensive and calm and in control. He thinks first, then he acts, and maybe later, he feels. My mother acts first, then she may think about it, and then she feels. When she feels first, watch out, it could get ugly.

Behavioral therapists say we must act first. Cognitive therapists say our thinking controls our feelings, which then control our actions. Me, I feel. I can't seem to help it. Beth's crying made me feel out of control with emotion. My buttons were being pushed. I could not stop what I was feeling; Sarah could not stop what she was feeling. Most of the time, I am pretty certain that people cannot change intense emotion when they are feeling it, at least not at the exact moment that they are feeling it.

Sarah was lucky she had to go to work, so was Martin. When she came home she was more ready and able to talk and to hear why Martin had condoms in his travel bag. Had she done so at the moment of finding them, it would have been a nasty fight.

If I had gone to Beth during her fit I probably would have said or done something regrettable. Of course, you have been there too. The lesson here is clear: If you ever feel some emotion too intensely, you must *act* first, get away, and come back later. You don't always have to deal with the situation at the moment the intense emotion is present. Frankly, it seems clear to me that we should do whatever we can to come back to the story at a later time. Get away! Create some distance, take some time by controlling the part of you that is controllable—and that's your behavior or your action—because controlling your thinking and your feelings can sometimes be impossible, just ask Sarah, Martin, Beth, or me.

18

Fool's Gold

Finding out that there's a better way to treat people than by following the Golden Rule wasn't as shocking as finding out about Santa Claus, the Tooth Fairy or that tilting your head back to stop a nose bleed was wrong. It was more difficult to understand though. After all, "Do unto others as you would have them do unto you" was the mantra of countless Sunday school teachers, kindergarten teachers and parents when I was young. It's a good rule, not a great rule. George Bernard Shaw once said, "Do not do unto others as you would that they should do unto you. Their tastes may not be the same."

Here's a minor example: Megan hates to have her picture taken, refuses to allow it, has gone as far as cutting her image out of a photo that inadvertently caught her. Sofia *loves* to have her picture taken, will go to great lengths to get her likeness into photos. If Sofia were to do unto Megan as she has others do unto her, then she would think nothing of taking Megan's picture, even though Megan *hates* to have her picture taken.

Alma and Barb are from two different cultural backgrounds. In Barb's culture, the concept of time is an amazingly precise thing. If you tell Barb to meet you somewhere at 1:00 p.m., Barb will be there at 12:55! If you invite Barb to dinner at your home, she will ask what time you want her there, and, she will arrive at exactly that time. If you tell Alma to meet you somewhere at 1:00, she almost never arrives by 1:00. In Alma's world, 1:00 is an estimation of a time. If something comes up at 12:50 (say, her best friend stops by or calls), she will take her time (which in Alma's world is infinite, not measurable, and not linear), talk to her friend and leave when they are done. If she invites someone to dinner and he or she ask, "What time?" She will tell them, "At dinner time." If there is a party and someone tells her the party is 8:00 to 11:00, Alma will wonder what happens at 11:00. If she is having fun, will they kick her (and the other guests) out of the house at that time? To Alma, having precise times for dinner or time spans for parties is rude. To Barb, Alma's late arrival to most meetings is rude. In reality, neither believes she is rude, but their perception is that the other is being inconsiderate. Conflict between these two women, on the issue of time, is inevitable. If Alma and Barb don't work this out, their relationship will end. Ironically, dealing with this conflict will build intimacy in their friendship. (I believe this is true for almost every relationship.)

If they were to follow the Golden Rule, Alma and Barb would be in a lot of conflict. There are many other examples of this. I am thinking about the dinner table at my house compared to some other homes. Our home is full of noise, talking, arguing and, teasing; manners are secondary to connecting verbally. Other homes value silence in a different way than we do in mine. If I were to do unto you, as I would have you do unto me, I would be very loud at your dinner table, you may be very quiet at mine, and neither of us would be very comfortable.

At a recent workshop on cross-cultural communication, Barb and Alma helped me (and the other participants) to examine how these differences permeate our lives in ways we would not even imagine. They brought up four volunteers and asked them each to demonstrate the "correct" way of folding a bath towel. Each volunteer, to my surprise, folded the towel differently. I was surprised because, 1) I didn't know there was that many ways to fold a towel, and 2) I wasn't aware of the passion inherent in each group of towel folders. Some of the audience even cheered for certain folding methods. To further illustrate this point, in a more dualistic or dichotomous way, Barb asked the audience what was the proper way to hang toilet paper, over or under? The energy around this issue was downright frightening.

On both of these fronts it is clear who is right. Everyone is. Perception is everything, and my perception is always right—to me—and your perception is always right to you. Our perceptions on many issues may not be the same. As one of my favorite Reader's Digest quotes once said, "If two people agree on everything, there's no need for one of them!"

The concept of knowing what is "best" for another, based on what is "best" for you, does not take *their* needs, views, culture or history into account. It assumes that my needs are identical to their needs.

So what is the better rule if the Golden Rule isn't best anymore? Some people call it the "Platinum Rule." Do unto others, as *they* would have you do unto them, not as you would have them do unto you. This way, each of us gets the choice to decide how we want to be "done unto." It is no longer about treating others your way—it's about treating them their way. So if I want you to replace my toilet paper and you like it under but I like it over, then you would put it over. Is that not a kinder, more empathic rule? At the very least, the Platinum Rule invites negotiation, compromise and discussion about different perceptions.

If I assume that I can know how you want me to conduct myself with you, based on how I desire you to conduct yourself with me, I am assuming that we are more alike than we may actually be—which may or may not be true depending on our values, our culture, our gender, or our history. And so today, I am not going to assume that I *know* how the people in my life want to be "done unto." I am going to engage in a dialogue to learn how they want me to be for them, not how I want them to be for me and assume that they are the same, because often, they are not.

Oh, and by the way, if you're ever at my house and the toilet paper needs replacing, I really do prefer it over, thank you very much.

19

Something In The Air

Sharon came to talk about her anger at her husband, Gary. Gary just didn't get it, Sharon complained. He worked all day, that was true, but she worked all day and night, and it just wasn't fair. Women have been saying this about men for years, and, by the sound of the women who come to talk to me in therapy, things haven't really changed much at all in the past fifty years!

Sharon wanted to know why it was her job to work all day, and then come home to feed and bathe the kids, and then clean up while Gary read the paper and watched the news. Women ask me this question all the time, as if I am the spokesperson for all men. As if they are searching to uncover some secret I keep that would get their husbands to help more.

"Why," they ask, "are men like that?"

"Simple," I would say, "It's their air. And they're (we're) used to the way it smells. It doesn't stink to us." You know how it goes: If you're in air that stinks for a long time, you stop noticing the smell of the air; it just becomes normal to you. Why should men change? It's our air and it doesn't smell to us.

When Sharon was through telling her story, I asked her what was Gary's motivation to change. The answer was clear. He had none. Everything was going his way. He had a beautiful wife who kept his house, took care of the kids, contributed to the family economy, and was a willing lover to boot. Why would he change? Life was great, for him. And people are just animals after all, so without motivation to change, Gary (or you or I) are unlikely to make any change at all.

This is the concept of *privilege*—the inability to smell the air when it stinks for someone other than you. Sometimes, the air doesn't seem to stink for me, but it stinks for others. The air I hear about the most is the polluted air of the "typical" American married woman.

Of course, there is other stinky air; women don't have the monopoly on breathing polluted air. It's hard work to notice when the air stinks for someone else, especially when it doesn't stink for you. Not only is it hard work, there's little motivation to notice it, because, who wants to smell stinky air if they don't have to?

I was riding my bike to a 7-11 in Powell, Ohio many years ago when I noticed that there was no wheelchair access ramp. I had to stop and lift my bike up to the store—which was no big deal for me, but would have been for my friend Rick, who is in a wheel chair. When I told the store manager that they needed a ramp, she yelled at me, "What are you worried about? You can walk!"

Learning to smell the air when it doesn't stink for me has been a blessing and a curse. The blessing is that I am more in touch with the plight of others and this helps me empathize and connect to people. The curse is that I can often feel pain that I would not have normally noticed. For example, hearing David Letterman tell "fat" people jokes bothers me, not because I'm fat (I'm not), but because it hurts people and there are better ways to be funny.

When Gary doesn't help his wife it hurts him as much as it hurts her, he just doesn't know it, nor can he understand why. I know, because he told me.

It is easier to not smell other people's air, but if any real change is ever going to happen for those less advantaged it will be necessary to start to smell the air when it stinks, especially when it doesn't stink to you. Taking time to notice the hurts that others may experience, especially when you are not in the position to suffer will lead you to understand the world through another person's eyes—or in this case, through another person's nose, by smelling the stink in the air.

It seems that the world would be a better place if we could get some cleaner air to breathe, and the pollution of oppression, anger, resentment, hatred and guilt could be washed away forever if those of us who have the ability to lift our bikes up over the curb would take some time to noticed how it would be for those who can't.

In the case of the 7-11 clerk who had to hear my rant, the air didn't smell to her, her legs worked just fine. She couldn't understand why I would be upset about not having a curb cut for a wheelchair and she wondered why it smelled to me. So, I called the corporate headquarters of Southland Corporation and two weeks later, they were cutting the curb for a ramp. I guess somebody heard me.

Taking time to smell the air especially when it doesn't stink for you will surely lead to change for those who are unfortunate enough to live in smelly air!

20

Cry Me A River

Sometimes, for no apparent reason, people just need to cry. Often, people are befuddled by this need and want to figure out why they're driven to tears. Why do we question our tears? It seems important that people simply allow themselves the freedom to feel what they feel, when they feel it. Trying to figure out *why* takes us away from the feeling, and perhaps the reason people are feeling *x or y* (sad or scared, for example) is because they have some unresolved emotion that has been waiting to get out. Trying to figure out *why* is a cognitive action, involving thinking, which often leads us away *from* the feeling, not toward it.

Men are especially good at thinking their feelings into submission, with themselves and with the women and children in their lives. It's as if crying or feeling any emotion is not okay. It's as if knowing why the feeling is coming out would solve some sort of problem, as if the emotion is the problem itself.

Sometimes in therapy, I listen to men ask women why they feel a certain way. I see them working very hard, not only to find out why, but to end the emotional outburst in some way. When people cannot *solve* the mystery of the emotion, they often get frustrated and angry with themselves, sending a message to the person who is emoting that what they are feeling is not okay.

One story that has always stayed with me involves a young couple that came to talk about the conflicts they had been dealing with. They wanted to learn healthy, more appropriate ways to deal with their differences. Usually, I'll ask a couple to discuss their conflict in front of me and I will work on teaching them some "techniques" for how to fight fair. This particular fight was about backpack camping. The man wanted to go backpack camping really badly, and he wanted to go with his wife. The wife didn't want to go and he *needed* to know why—as if any reason would've been enough! She told him she was afraid—no, *petrified*—of bears. She said her fear of bears made the idea of backpack camping repulsive to her.

He wanted to know why. So, she told him. She gave him five reasons why she was afraid of bears. Do you know what he did? He gave her ten reasons why she shouldn't be afraid of bears.

In this argument, she had to *prove* to him why she was afraid. It was as if the mere fact that she was afraid, regardless of her reason, wasn't enough.

When people are *forced* to address their specific reasons for an emotion, they are essentially being asked to PROVE *why* they feel what they feel—and this request to have to PROVE why you feel the way you feel often results in more frustration for the respondent. This dialogue rarely leads people to a better understanding and often leads to a bigger conflict. People seem to want cognitive, or (what seems to be) *rational* reasons explained to them regarding another person's emotional state. They want cognitive answers to an affective process. "You feel *what*!? *Why* do you feel that!?" The fact was, this woman was afraid of bears and it didn't matter how many (cognitive, rational) reasons to quell her fears her husband gave her; she was still going to be afraid of bears!

Feelings are always okay. Not only are they okay, they're essential to healthy growth. Some people even believe that one of the reasons men in the United States die eight years younger than women, on average, is they don't allow themselves the freedom to express their feelings as freely as they could.

Men are socialized to "fix" things when they are broken. Feelings often cannot be fixed; feelings, often, just are. They are the free, unabashed expression of something that is going on inside. Knowing why is not necessarily the way to fix the feelings. Perhaps feelings don't have to be fixed.

Julie has a four-year-old daughter, Kayla, who has been crying a lot lately. Kayla's father recently moved out of the home and Julie knows that this is "why" Kayla has been crying. Kayla knows, too. This hasn't stopped the crying, any more than having ten reasons not to be afraid of bears stopped one woman's fear of bears.

The work appears to be to allow the feelings to come out. Recently, I saw a man in my office who started his first session by stating he had been feeling violent lately. So violent, in fact, he had the impulse to kill his roommate. When asked what his roommate was doing that would lead to him feeling like he could kill him, the man said, "Just his breathing could make me want to kill him some days. He's really a nice man, it's not him, it's me!"

This man had some feelings he needed to get out. This is the same phenomenon as Kayla and the woman who was afraid of bears.

People are a lot like trash compactors: They can hold a lot of trash, but even a trash compactor cannot hold all the trash in the world. Even trash compactors have to be emptied sometimes, if for no other reason than they are full. Knowing what each specific piece of trash is won't change the fact that the can is full and must be emptied.

All three of the people in this story had a lot of trash that needed emptying. The homicidal man looked like he was going to explode when he sat down in my office, and someday he might. I hope not. Kayla was exploding, everyday. Julie was getting frustrated listening to Kayla dump her trash. The work here is clear to me: People gather lots of trash and sometimes they need to dump it. If the trash does not get taken out regularly the can will explode and somebody could get hurt. There is nothing to fix about trash needing to be taken out ... there's no reason needed to find out why people cry or feel a particular emotion. Mostly, it's because we are people, and people feel—and that's okay, as long as we allow ourselves to do so.

So cry me a river, and don't worry about answering why. Today, allow the most honest aspect of yourself to just feel what it feels. You can try to figure out why you feel this way tomorrow, *after* you've taken out the trash.

21

Misery Loves Company?

Pain is an amazingly relative thing. Often, the people I meet in therapy try to compare their pain to another person's, but that isn't really possible. The reality is that each of us has the opportunity to make, feel, and experience our own pain(s) in life, and not anyone else's.

A fascinating phenomenon occurs—especially in group therapy—when people are thrust together to work on their issues or problems with others. This forum of therapy relies on the philosophy that misery loves company; but what I've observed from this end of the couch is this generality is not quite true. Misery does not love all company at all. Misery, it seems, loves company *that's also miserable!* Misery hates company that isn't also miserable (check it out the next time you're not feeling too well).

Suzanne felt like she was going crazy. She wasn't, but it didn't matter, because she *felt* as if she was. She came to group therapy to gain the sense that she was not the only one whose anxiety was so great that the "voice" inside her head led her to think she was nuts. (I should note here that we all have a voice in our head, the voice *talks* to us, it's called thinking!)

During the group's first meeting, Elizabeth took time to share some of her story. She told the group of an abusive childhood and horribly painful stories of her father's alcohol abuse and how it affected her. She told us one especially sad story of being left to wait for him after "the big game" in which she was named captain of the cheerleaders. He had promised her that he would be there. She "drew us a picture" of what it was like for her to assure her friends that he *would* be there, and then to find herself sitting alone on a curb after everyone had gone, crying and waiting for him. When he eventually arrived, he was drunk and she couldn't ask where he had been or why he hadn't come—she had to "take care of him" and ask him if he was okay. (We call the action of kids taking care of their parents *"parentification."*)

During the second week of group, Kyle told his story; it too was sad. People don't usually come to therapy to talk about the good things in their life; they come to share the bad news. (Actually, it's a good thing that the *news* which people share is bad, that's what makes it *news*. I am reminded of my eighth grade social studies teacher who, when asked why the news is always bad replied, "When the news we watch on TV is more good than bad, then we will be in real trouble! That's why it is news. When *good* becomes news, we will really have to worry.") Anyhow, Kyle shared his story of finding out that he had cancer in his leg and the doctors told him that they might have to amputate it to keep it from spreading to the rest of his body. Kyle was only 18 years old.

Rick was in a wheelchair. He couldn't walk at all. He told us his story of having been a brash and brave teenager of 15 when he and a group of his buddies ran to the swimming hole and he was the first to dive in, banging his head on a rock and paralyzing him for life. Rick was 27 when he was in my group and told this story. He had (mostly) forgiven himself for his foolishness.

Suzanne had pulled her chair away from the circle of the group and she sat quietly, listening. She didn't know what to say. She looked like she wasn't going to say anything—her pain couldn't compare to the pain of cancer, childhood abuse or being a quadriplegic. Suzanne still felt like she was going crazy on a daily basis, she feared that one day the thoughts in her head would go out of control and she would have to be taken away. She had thought about this scenario since she was a little kid. Others in the group were quiet too. One woman whose husband had just left her, one whose 14-year-old dog had recently died, another who struggled to find any relationship at all. After Kyle, Elizabeth and Rick shared their stories, the rest of the group got quiet. It was not an unusual thing for this silence to befall a group—it happened almost every time I ran a group; I knew it would happen this time too.

People were comparing pain. Suzanne, Joseph, Mary and Hillary didn't think that they could tell their stories. After all, what right did they have to say anything? Their problems were nothing compared to the others'. One thing *was* true though: everyone's pain was uniquely their own. They got to carry it into the group and they got to carry it out, just like Kyle, Elizabeth and Rick. Somehow, it seemed that the pain of these other members was not worthy after hearing about the traumas already shared. Apparently, misery only loves company when the misery is at least somewhat equal.

There's something funny about the emotional, physical and spiritual pain that resides inside each of us: The 'funny' thing is that you get to keep and do what you will with your pain, and you get relatively little to do with the pain of others. My pain is my pain, yours is yours. It's really quite simple. When given the opportunity to share your pain, in the presence of compassionate others, with people who not only "get" your pain but who are also willing to share their own with you—people begin to heal; to feel better; to feel like they matter and that they are appreciated. We don't take the pain away in therapy, we give it a place to breathe and be accepted—without judgment, just because it is real, genuine and worthy of attention.

Whenever the phenomenon of some people talking and some people sitting silently happens in group therapy, I always ask what is keeping the others from sharing, I ask even though I know what it is; in therapy terms I call it "the Colombo approach."

Members will often say they have no right to feel bad about their *measly* problems in life. So, I tell this silly story. I ask the members what it would be like for them if Kyle came in to group one day and his leg was amputated from the knee down; I ask what it would be like if, on that same day, when walking out of group they accidentally bumped their big toe into the door jam, bumped it hard! Would the toe feel pain? Would you scream out, "OUCH!?" The answer, of course, is yes. I then ask if they would be allowed to feel that pain? Could they stop the pain? Remember, Kyle has no leg. Does his lack of a leg take away your pain? Does repressing your pain help Kyle?

Your pain is yours; my pain is mine. It doesn't really help me if you keep your pain private out of respect for mine. Just because I have misery in my life, no matter how great that misery is doesn't mean that you don't also have misery or pain.

Suzanne eventually spoke in the group. She found out that others not only have felt the same way, but also some actually felt that way now. The group got to talk about the different pains they felt and somehow this helped them deal with, understand, and learn about themselves. It didn't fix anything, not really. It didn't take Rick out of his chair or get Elizabeth's dad to show up on time, but it did move people to see that it was up to them to deal with their own stubbed toes and not feel bad that their hurt wasn't as bad as someone else's.

In this process of shared misery we get to connect, to feel important and to see that we are not alone—even though in the midst of our pain, in the privacy of our hell, sometimes it might feel that way. In group therapy the connection between the members is the medicine we get to take and this leads members to feel hopeful and ready to tackle whatever their issues might be. It appears to me that when people in misery share their hurts with others who are also in pain, their wounds somehow start to heal.

22

Just Do It?

As a young child I was always fascinated by commercials and advertisements; I still am, as an adult. I have vivid memories of the old Alka Seltzer commercial that went "Plop, plop, fizz, fizz. Oh, what a relief it is!" Alka Seltzer had some of the best commercials, including one where all you could see was people's stomachs and someone tapping on another's stomach while they spoke, while catchy music played in the background. Another one that stuck in my house was the line, "Mama mia, *that's a **spicy** meatball!*"

Commercials have always caught my attention, good ones anyway. Many commercials seem to last through the years, with jingles and phrases becoming a part of popular culture. Perhaps the most popular single phrase in commercials during the past 30 years—indeed, perhaps the most popular marketing campaign in history—has been the phrase used by the Nike Company, "Just Do It." This motto became so popular and so tied to this company that they simply had to place their logo, the Swoosh, directly above or below these three words and they had an ad—an ad that has lasted a very long time.

Why was this ad so popular? How could it be that these three simple words stuck in the public conscience and became so successful that it has lasted for decades? Kids like it, adults like it, it appears to be equally popular with men and women, and it has even been translated into other languages and been successful in other countries.

As a person who works in the field of studying and helping people make change in their lives, this phrase stuck with me. When I was young, the philosophy my parents shared—especially my mother's philosophy—was essentially, quit complaining and just do it! I think the people at Nike must have known that this phrase, this philosophy, was somehow woven into the fabric of the American way.

But something has always bothered me about this phrase: I think the people at advertising campaign employed by Nike (like a lot of advertising companies) misled us. I'm not saying that the people at Nike lied, but they forgot to tell us the entire truth. They misled us by wanting us to believe that it was as simple as "Just Do It." They led us to think all we had to do was try (and buy their shoes) in order to achieve, and I think this message is misleading or only partially correct. As a psychologist, I think this motto may have led to people feeling guilty and poorly about themselves, especially when they couldn't "just do it" and didn't know why. In one commercial, Spike Lee used to comment: "It's GOTTA be the shoes!" after watching Michael Jordan do something amazing while wearing his Nikes. I'm certain that Nike didn't think I'd think I could *really* "be like Mike."

It seems that the people at Nike meant well and their phrase/philosophy is a good one, heck, it's a great one, that's why it has lasted so long and been embedded into the culture. What they didn't tell us was that Just Do It isn't enough. Bo Jackson (one of the first spokespeople for the Just Do It campaign) didn't just do it. Bo was amazing, the first well-marketed two-sport superstar, football AND baseball! He was a hero. (His black and white bat behind the back with shoulder pads on baseball card is still my favorite card of all time.) How did Bo do it? Did he just … do it? Why can't I just do it? Why can't you?

Well, it's simple: Nike lied, a little. Nobody can just do it, that's too simple. Good for selling shoes, not so effective for accomplishing things in life. People want an event, something fast, quick results … I want that too … it just isn't like that in real life. Just Do It is fine really; it's just not the entire process. Unfortunately, the ***process*** is more complicated. Just Do It is the 4th step in a five-step process, Nike didn't tell us that. For the sake of selling shoes, they told us that we could all skip to the good part. And, I agree mostly: we *can* shoot for our own gold medal moments, if we figure out the process. Here's the one I came up with for me:

Step I. You have to **want** to do it.
Step II. You have to **believe** you can do it.
Step III. You have to **figure out** what actions you're going to take to do it.
Step IV. **Just do it.**
Step V. Evaluate how you did, now that you did it.

There it is. Not *that* much more complicated than the Nike people said, but it is a process and not an event, just like most everything else. Plug your ideas into this formula … see what happens, whether it is changing your diet, getting on an exercise schedule, going back to school, working on your relationship(s), or for me today, writing this book. Each step is crucial, but Step II—believing that you can do it—is the one where most people get stuck. So, today, whatever your goal is, take 24 hours just to believe that you can do it. Try *those* shoes on, wear that idea around your life, and tomorrow, plug in the rest.

23

Hey Buddy, Can You Spare A Dime?

I used to envy physically beautiful people—men and women, little boys and little girls. I don't envy them anymore. They seem to get things too easily in life and that isn't really very helpful, not really.

One of those news magazine shows that once over-populated the nightly TV prime-time spots (Dateline, 20-20 and 60 Minutes) conducted an experiment in which two different women (actually, I think it was the same woman with different make-up) had a flat tire on a very busy city street. Of course, there were hidden cameras (thank you, Alan Funt) and viewers got to observe people react to this woman in their most natural, unabashed state. In one scenario, the woman is homely and obese. We witness her struggling to fix her tire. Passersby offer her little or no help; it's a very disturbing scene, especially since more of us look like this woman than the second woman, who is beautiful, of course.

Like most social psychology experiments done in "natural environments" it is not difficult to guess what happens to the beautiful woman. In this scene we witness people (mostly men, as I recall) practically running to help her. We even see one man check her out from a third story window before coming down to the street to help this *poor* woman.

I don't envy her. What did she do to get so much help? I don't envy the homely woman either, but at least she'll learn how to change a tire.

In elementary schools and on the athletic fields we can also see "good-looking" boys and girls getting special benefits. This doesn't seem to help them in the long *drive* through life. Many of the attractive clients I've counseled use their precious time in therapy confused about their self concept, wondering if it is *"them"* that people like or if it is the *"car"* they get to drive around in. Once, in a group therapy meeting there was this incredibly naïve and beautiful woman. She spoke often of her confusion about why she never had any good relationships with other women. Finally, after weeks of this confusion I said to the group, "Perhaps it's just me, but it appears obvious why other women struggle with you. Does anyone else see what that might be?" At this, every other member of the group slowly began to shake their heads yes. I asked if anyone would be willing to tell Jessica what it might be. And with that, first one man, and then a woman member stated directly, *"Jessica, for goodness sakes! You're beautiful!"* And then, without prompting, Jessica started to cry and explain that she was "never very pretty," that she looked "just like her father!" Jessica was not ready to admit that it was her looks, and not her personality that prevented her from having the relationships she wanted. Some envied her while others hated her—but either way, they weren't relating to her, but to how she looked—and this, was relatively, unchangeable.

It seems only natural that we often react to others based on how they look. Sometimes I wonder if we are even aware that we act differently around people to whom we are attracted (and not attracted).

As an adolescent I recall not having any trouble talking, laughing, and being myself around most people, unless I was around women to whom I was attracted. Then, I turned into a tongue-tied, nervous, awkward goof. I was like the men who ran to help the beautiful woman with her flat tire, acting like an idiot without thinking or knowing how to control it.

Teachers, coaches and parents who, unconsciously, "give" to kids because of how they look are not really helping them. This behavior teaches a terrible lesson, not only to the child, but also to the others watching. It teaches the handsome boy he is valued for something he cannot control. It teaches the adorable girl that *who* she is doesn't earn affection, but *how* she looks does.

Of all the insecure patients I have seen in therapy, the most insecure are the physically beautiful ones. For years I struggled to understand this phenomenon. The women worry and wonder why other women hate them. They are wounded, not only by the actions of the attentive males in their lives, but also by the females who may avoid or ignore them. They struggle to find out who they are and what they can be, regardless of their appearance. This struggle often causes people to act out in ways to prove that they are more than just 'how they look.' They may engage in behaviors that lead to overachievement to prove their worth or underachievement to prove that they are "just like everyone else." Either way, they are forced to ask questions that an 'average' looking person may never have to struggle with.

Handsome men get the attention of women and become the envy of other males. They sometimes believe more highly of themselves than their actual 'real' accomplishments suggest they have earned. This may lead them to not try as hard due to their false belief that they are more successful in life than they really are. Often, the attention they get causes men to take the women they're dating for granted. They may fail to work to deepen their relationships and their commitments to relationships. They may believe that the women they date are replaceable since there are often other women getting in line to have the *trophy man*, so they can be the envy of their friends.

I don't wish too much beauty on my children. I want them to earn what they get, and not have to compensate for their deficiencies by striving to be more physically beautiful. Being too attractive seems more like a curse than a blessing in the long run. When young couples come to my office for counseling to improve their relationship I often ask why they are together, what attracts them to each other? Too often to count, I hear them say they are together because she or he is so beautiful. This answer scares me, and it should scare them. Two things that don't seem to last in life are youth and traditional physical beauty. If we are lucky enough to live a long time, these two things will leave us. Eventually, gravity sets, our looks change dramatically and if we're lucky, we get old.

In my quest to be a better person I have attempted to examine how I act toward all people regardless of how they look. I noticed that I flirted more with cute women and was more business-like with men. I noticed that I talked differently to people based on my perception of their economic background, racial make-up or ethnicity. I found that this chameleon-like behavior followed me to other situations as well. In my search for being a genuine, consistent person I have attempted to see who and how I am around all people, even the beautiful ones. As I strive to become a better human being I have found that I want to help everyone with a flat tire, not just the pretty ones.

I wonder what that says about me when I find myself acting differently with people based solely on how they look. Sounds rather shallow doesn't it? Interesting too, that in the end, the behavior is helpful to no one. It seems that my behavior is actually my attempt to find ways to connect with people—to feel closer and have a sense of familiarity that creates some kind of bond between us, like two Harley-

Davidson motorcyclists acknowledging each other as they ride past one another. Perhaps in my attempts to make some kind of connection with others I can look for (and find) something more significant to grab onto than how someone looks and I can strive to reach deeper as I connect to who a person is. And maybe, by being more of myself, when I finally do connect, it will be a more genuine me who is reaching out with that connection.

24

Fred Flintstone Feet

My feet *were* my best physical characteristic.

As sad as it is that feet could be a "best" characteristic, I must admit, it *was* true ... and the worst part is, I can't say it is *still* true.

I have a long and close history with my feet and toes. It's different than most peoples' story. The family tale goes something like this:

I was born about one month earlier than my intended due date and I was the second son of a teen-age mother, arriving ten short months after my brother was born. When I was born I was very little and frail and so, of course, my mother was very scared that something would be wrong with me. So, while she was not surprised when the doctor returned to the room to tell her the bad news of my health, she was terribly upset at what she heard. The doctor came into the room and said, "Mrs. Benn, we have some bad news for you—not terrible, this problem is fixable!" Then, a nurse brought me into the room and showed my mother my toes, which were webbed, stuck together between the second and the third toe. The doctor continued, "His toes are webbed, but we can have them cut apart."

At which time my mother proclaimed, "DON'T TOUCH THEM! THEY'RE SO CUTE, I LOVE THEM."

This is the story of my incredibly cute toes. I was raised to love my toes and my feet and I always saw them as better than other people's toes and feet. My second toe, while stuck to my third toe, is shorter than my big toe, as I think toes should be. The rest of my toes follow suit and each one, in order, is smaller than the one next to it. Perfect toes, perfect feet. The web makes them more unique. I always loved my feet, hence, they became my favorite feature. That doesn't make you want to see the rest of me, does it?

My toes were always an interesting and fun story to tell at a party. Sometimes my friends would tell people about them and I'd be forced to take off my shoes and show my toes. It was very funny. One time, while I was at the local pool with my brother, he nudged me as we stood in line at the concession stand, showing me the person next to me, staring with amazement at my freaky toes.

Sometimes I would tell people that they "run in my family because my stepmother has them too." And they would say, "Oh," not quite getting the humor in it ... even though it's true, she does. Other times I would tell people I was disqualified from the Olympic time trials the year that Mark Spitz won the seven gold medals due to an unfair advantage. I tell them I even beat Mark Spitz, and they are not sure whether to believe me or not. I can be a pretty convincing liar—I mean, storyteller.

Well, my toes and I are now pretty old. Like many middle class Americans, I've had a rich life full of hard work, schooling, raising kids and having the kind of troubles that make life full.

I always thought I knew about things. I thought I knew what to do for my children, my family and my work. I figured if I worked hard and did good deeds, things would go well. I also always thought I had great feet. One day, while I was hunting for shoes with my wife, I commented to the clerk on how great my feet were, how they were perfectly shaped and all (I hadn't even mentioned the webbed toes) when my wife jumped in and said, "Are you kidding? You think you have nice feet? Mark, you have Fred Flintstone feet! They're perfectly square, just like on the Flintstones!"

Wow ... she was right. I have Fred Flintstone feet. Perfectly square, not normal, more like a cartoon character than a man. The bubble was burst. In one fell swoop, one comment, one look, one snicker, one chuckle, one moment, my best feature was gone. And, worse than that, I don't have another feature to replace it with. I am reduced to having no favorite feature, not one.

Also, coincidentally, something even more disturbing happened in my life. My third son was caught lying, cheating, stealing, doing drugs and essentially betraying his mother and me. It hit me as fast as my favorite feature disappeared. I thought I knew my son, I thought I knew about parenting, I thought I was "doing good" and as a result I would do well. And now, today, I am not so sure that I know anything. I don't know about my son, my understanding about parenting, the world, my daughters, my work or anything else I thought I knew and understood.

I want to go back to those parties with my friends, to that pool with that person staring at my feet. I want to see the world the way it used to be. I want people to think that maybe I really did beat Mark Spitz and then got disqualified for having an unfair advantage with my webbed toes. I want to have another new best feature, and sometimes I am afraid that I never will.

I am afraid that I never will ... I feel lost in the woods somehow and when you are lost in the woods, the last thing you should do is run, lest you risk getting even more lost. So I sit with my fear of not having a favorite characteristic, and of not knowing anything; and I listen to the fear to see what it was there to teach. And this is what I am learning: sometimes life throws you things you cannot understand and you may not be prepared for. Sometimes, having pain and sadness and fear is good. Without the pain the lessons are diluted and less powerful. So, learning that my feet were like Fred Flintstone's wasn't all bad—now, instead of perfect, my feet are funny—and really, I guess they always were; and there are a lot worse things than having funny Fred Flintstone Feet.

Oh, and my son, well … the pain was there to teach him too. It taught him that he has a serious problem that needed to be corrected—and his "cry for help" while painful was what led us all to know that he was lost in the woods. Maybe it had to happen so we could find him to help him out and teach him about how not to get so lost the next time he thinks to go there.

25

Don't Care TOO Much

It was a beautifully sunny, cool autumn day. We were visiting Mike and Deb Warner in Pittsburgh, PA. Deb and Mike had two sons at the time, and we had three boys of our own so visiting with them and their boys was like visiting "the cousins." Watching these boys getting together to play was almost as fun for the adults as it was for the kids. When they were together they went crazy, doing all the things that give parents fits of fear that someone is going to get hurt. I am certain the kind of play these boys got into led to parental warning phrases such as, *"you're going to break your neck or you're going to poke somebody's eye out or somebody's gonna get hurt!"* These standard expressions come with the Parenting Handbook that parents subconsciously receive when they leave the hospital with their newborn babies. Often, the Warner boys and our sons would go outside and play for hours, and this was the perfect day for that. This setup worked well for us parents—their playing outside provided plenty of kid-free time to engage in adult conversations about politics, sports, relationships, other people, and sex. It was time that adult parents crave and made the three-hour round-trip journey to Deb and Mike's house worth it!

The four older boys whose ages ranged between three and eight interrupted the flow of our 'adult conversation' often, making it difficult to stay on track and engage in discussions consistently; as parents, we were used to this and learning to deal with frequent interruption was just a part of the job of parenting. So, when Zach, the Warner's oldest son came in shouting that the boys had decided they wanted to go bike riding we were all pretty happy with that idea, thinking that perhaps we'd actually get some uninterrupted time to be grown-ups, a rare event in any family with young children.

Pittsburgh, if you haven't been there, is very hilly, and not a very safe place to ride bikes for little kids. Anyhow, in an effort to squeeze in some childless adult time, we allowed the boys to go off and ride around the safe suburbs of Pittsburgh, Pennsylvania. Of course, this was a big mistake, or there would be no story to tell. And, if the truth were told, I had an uneasy feeling in my gut about the boys taking off and riding in the neighborhood terrain of Pittsburgh. I am usually pretty good at listening to my "silent harm alarm" that lives inside my body somewhere, but on this day, my craving for some kid-free time must've overwhelmed this feeling.

The kids were gone for about an hour when the phone rang … it was one of those *"premonition phone calls."* When the phone rang Barb and I shot a quick glare at each other, and I could almost hear her sigh as she glanced over at me with her jaw dropped and her hand covering her mouth as if to say, "oh crap, something happened." It was uncanny how we both felt this as the phone sounded the alarm to step into action. We both seemed to sense that this call was bad news coming and we were right.

The Price family was calling to say that our son Jesse (the five-year-old) was lying in front of their house. They were keeping him immobile; they told us that they "had stopped the bleeding, covered him with a blanket and were waiting for us before taking any other action."

In a rare and bizarre state of panic, I took off running for their house, even though I wasn't sure where I was going. Deb said it was down the hill and to the left, about two blocks. I didn't want to wait for the car, so I ran. I ran until I saw this kid lying on a sidewalk with a group of spectators gathered around. It didn't look good, and being out of breath from running and the adrenalin-rush, I arrived at the scene wanting to take charge and assess the situation.

When I got to Jesse I took time to calm myself and did a survey of his abilities. I asked him if he could feel his feet, move his toes, lift his arm. Clearly, he had not injured anything permanently, at least nothing spinal. The relief I felt was overwhelming, it calmed me completely.

Deb got her car and I carried my injured kindergartner to it. I sat him on my lap in the front seat and sang to him softly as we drove to the hospital. He had a minor laceration on his chin that required a few stitches, but he complained during the drive about his jaw and how much it hurt. Upon arrival to the emergency room, I told the attendants I thought his jaw was broken. They told me a broken jaw was unlikely for a child of five, and they reluctantly x-rayed him. I knew it was broken long before the results came back; Jesse was a tough kid, and he wouldn't have complained about the jaw instead of the blood, unless the jaw was severely hurt.

Jesse's jaw was indeed broken and he would have to endure numerous trips to the orthodontist to make certain it was growing right, which it eventually did.

During one of our trips to the doctor, Jesse confronted me about my behavior the day of the accident. Through tears of anger he asked me, "Why didn't you care about me the day I got hurt? Why were you so calm? Didn't you see how hurt I was?!"

This line of questioning was almost comical to me as I reflected on MY experience that day and how hard I had to work to stay calm as I attempted to soothe my son's fears while I held him and we drove in Deb's car to the hospital. I had learned early in life that staying calm in the face of crisis was an essential ingredient to making good decisions and helping the situation. Panic was never very helpful and I had seen many people panic in the face of crisis and had witnessed how useless and destructive it can be. I remember being calm on the outside (for Jesse and Deb) and shaking on the inside. I even recall singing and humming to him on the way to the hospital and acting casually in my attempt to help soothe my injured child. I stayed very calm when I told the ER attendants to x-ray my son even though they didn't think it was necessary and I recall thinking that they may not have taken me seriously if I had been acting like a frightened parent.

What's funny is I was staying as calm as I could during this 'crisis' but it wasn't because I "didn't care" … it was because I knew that everything that was damaged that day was fixable, and because I DID care!

Most *everyday* crises are fixable, and things that are fixable are not worth freaking out about. Jesse was scared to death that day; I was too, until I reached him and saw that he was okay. Freaking out and worrying are as American as apple pie … so are heart attacks and ulcers. Me, I don't want to die young or suffer along the way, so I'm going to do what I can to stay calm in the face of perceived crisis. I am going to react with calm as often as possible; I just hope that I don't have to practice too often, along the way toward old age.

But if you see someone acting calm and controlled in the face of a crisis, it probably doesn't mean that they don't care, it most likely means that they do.

26

Act As If …

You and I are dying. Yes, that's right. I don't mean to get depressing about this, but it's true, life is terminal. We're all dying. In the United States, some people get to reach their normal life expectancy of 70 to 80 years; some don't make it that long. Regardless, I am acutely aware I will be dead very soon, no matter how many years, months, days or minutes I get. In one of his songs Jackson Browne says, "In the end it's the wink of an eye."

I'm afraid Jackson is right, and I am very aware I am going to die. What's weird about my awareness is the lack of sadness or depression I am feeling about it right now. In some ways I think it is good to know life is terminal, and that I am dying (slowly, I hope) even as I type these words. That knowledge will help me today by encouraging me to grab and appreciate as many moments as I can, especially when I am aware they are finite.

Ira Blount didn't know his life was finite when he died. I don't think Chris Harrington did either. Chris and Ira didn't know each other, but I knew them when they died and, through their deaths, each of them made an impact on my life that still affects me today. I learned about Chris and Ira years apart, but in the same hallways of my high school. Somebody from your high school died too, I'm sure of it. If you are not yet in high school, get ready—somebody from your school will probably die too. The depressing part is that someone will die before his or her time; it almost always happens, or so it seems. And, depending on fate, luck, misfortune or genetics it could be you or someone very close to you.

Chris died in a plane crash, a few years after Ira; Ira died the way most young people in the United States die, in a car wreck. I attended both funerals and saw Chris and Ira for the last time on the day they were buried. Both times the churches overflowed with mourners. I don't recall anything about the service except Chris and Ira's black hair had turned somewhat gray and people were crying. And they were dead. I got that. There is something about young people dying that hits home like nothing else, and their death was a haunting reminder to me that I was as mortal as anyone else.

It's one thing to realize as a teenager that you're mortal, but quite another to process and fully comprehend that information, or to know what to do with it in your adolescent mind. I mourned my friends and got on with my life, never appreciating how their deaths might continue to impact how I lived. But life continues to teach us the same lessons until we can hear them, and my repeat lesson came a few years ago. Three days before my 3rd son was to get his driver's license, he and a group of three friends took our 1994 Nissan Pathfinder down the street to fetch some food from one friend's house. While driving, a deer jumped out in front of the car, and my son turned the vehicle and flew off a 350-foot steep cliff. The car did not roll. The car did not explode. The car was somehow tethered to the earth in one of those miracles of life that cannot be explained and will make the hairs on the back of your neck stand up if you were to stand at the spot where they drove off. The car landed and spun, tires and windows exploded and four teenage boys sat at the bottom of a cliff, dazed and shocked, wondering if they were really alive and had survived the *"unsurvivable."*

My son was completely unharmed. But I was reminded again that this time we have is *"the wink of an eye"* and when I drive by the spot where he went off the cliff every morning on my way to work, I breathe a silent thanks that his story did not end like Chris and Ira's. Sometimes I stop the car and look over the ridge, to remind myself to be thankful for the life that was given to him, and to me. The good part about being aware of the fact that life is terminal has become clear to me: Since life is finite, it behooves me to drink up each minute, enjoy life, and try not to hurt anybody. I try to take time in each action, during the limited days I get to ask myself if the specific step I are currently taking will lead closer to where I want to go (literally or figuratively), or take me further from it. I try to take time to examine whether the world would be a better place if I were to move in this direction or worse. That's the philosophy I try to live by and what I teach my clients, my students and my children.

Because disasters happen. Miracles too. Each of these stories of teenage boys living and dying has taught me this—and I refuse to take these lessons for granted by honoring Chris and Ira who died, and Andrew and his friends, who didn't. I want to live this day and be thankful that I've got it, because I don't have a minute to waste ... and neither do you.

27

Welcome to Adulthood

We've all heard the saying, *"Youth is wasted on the young."* I think they're right, (whoever *they* are) although I wasn't sure until I became an adult. I don't think I understood; unfortunately, now that I'm old(er) I think I do.

My oldest son (who was 17 at the time) called me at work when he was in 11th grade. It was the middle of the workday, around noon. He didn't even say hello. In his angriest voice he said, *"I'm stuck at Wendy's with some friends and your piece of crap car won't start, what should I do?"* This kind of event is every parent's dream or nightmare, depending on your mood. This memory makes me laugh just thinking about it. I probably chuckled to myself while listening to my son cry to me about his dilemma. He was very upset and he wanted me to fix it; he wanted me to fix it in the same way a very young child who is blinded by the sun will ask their parents to 'turn off the sun' for them. Kids often think their parents can (and should) fix everything for them. I remember thinking that my parents could fix everything for me too, back when youth was being wasted on me.

In an unrelated incident, one of my doctoral students spoke to me this morning about the financial pressures he and his fiancée have shouldered during the past six months. You know, the usual stuff: They bought a house, a car, furniture and a dog. Like many soon-to-be and newly married people, Geoff and his girlfriend bit off more than they could chew, probably under the childish impression that somebody would take care of it for them—like my son Josh must have felt when he called about the car not starting. In addition, the fiancée had taken a job she disliked, but couldn't quit, since she was paying all the bills while Geoff was in graduate school.

Both stories are equally sad and amusing to me. That's how these stories are, they can be sad and amusing if somebody else is dealing with it and not you—especially if it *was* you at an earlier time, somewhere between youth and *real* adulthood. I think *real* adulthood comes *after* living through events like these; at least it did for Josh, Geoff and me.

Both Geoff and Josh were dealing with important emancipation issues that lead to adulthood and both stories are similar because in both situations we see young adults who are stuck. They are stuck with the opportunity and challenge to figure it out. Stuck with having the prospect of learning first-hand the lesson that most adults learn: sometimes adulthood sucks. At the very least, it isn't all it was cracked up to be.

When I was a kid, wasting time not enjoying my youth, all I ever wanted was to be a grown up. It looked so free and easy—getting to make all the decisions you want, seemingly nobody to answer to—what could be better?

Well, ask Geoff and Josh, or any young person on the verge of stepping into real adulthood. Both Geoff and Josh were at different phases on the path toward emancipation, each learning important lessons about how to cope when mom or dad can't turn off the sun.

The heat of adulthood can be oppressive. For Josh, on this day, he found his father unsympathetic. He heard me say, "*Wow, bummer Josh, jeez, whattaya gonna do? Stuck at Wendy's, car won't start?*

Hmmm, how are you going to get back to school? No, I can't come and get you; I have clients to see and class to teach, and by the way, good luck son. And, oh yeah, one more thing, welcome to adulthood, sometimes it sucks."

For Geoff, the same story applied, just bigger problems than how to find a way to get back to school, but solvable problems nonetheless. Both of these young men are leaping into adulthood, emancipating from the world of having their problems solved for them. That's what adulthood is, learning how to figure things out for yourself, nobody coming to rescue you.

It is hard, you know? I mean, how are we suppose to learn ways to solve our problems when, during our *ignorance-is-bliss-years*, all of our problems are either solved, coaxed, or coached to a workable solution by people who care about us?

I tried to help both of these young men this week; I tried to help them by *not* helping them. Actually, I think that's the best thing I could've done. Welcome to adulthood. If you're lucky, you didn't get too much help along the way so that by the time it's up to you to figure it out on your own, you'll know what to do.

28

Blessings in Disguise

It seems that everything is both blessing and curse, everything. Nothing is as simple as being completely one or the other.

In 1998 I spoke at a candlelight vigil for Matthew Shepard, the gay man who was beaten to death by two men in Laramie, Wyoming. More than 500 people showed up in support of this young man. On the night of his murder, Matthew Shepard had been doing nothing more than enjoying his life.

I didn't know Matthew Shepard, but he was my friend, my neighbor, my brother, and my son. Matthew Shepard was you and Matthew Shepard was me. Matthew Shepard died at 21 for no fault of his own.

During the weekend that Matthew lay dying in bed at the hospital down the street from my home, my 11-year-old son sat crying at our kitchen table, wondering why such cruelty had to happen. He told me that he wished he could sit with a prejudice person and ask him or her, simply, "Why?" He wondered aloud why people hate for no apparent reason. I wanted to tell him why. I even tried. Then, I realized I couldn't find the words. Nothing I could say would make sense of what had happened. What has happened thousands of times throughout our violent American history. The very same thing that has happened in very many ways to Blacks, Hispanics, women, children, Jews, the elderly, people with disabilities, Asians, Native Americans and to gays, lesbians, bisexuals and transgender people. No words. None.

Nothing I could say to help ease my little boy's pain and fear. Nothing I could do to ease the pain of Mr. and Mrs. Shepard, who had lost their only son.

Often, in times of death and tragedy, we are moved to silence. On the night of Matthew Shepard's vigil, silence wouldn't do. It was time to find a voice to speak out against hatred and anger. To speak up and declare that, just for one night, Matthew Shepard could represent all of the senseless deaths that have come from hate for no apparent reason—at least, no reason I could understand and explain to my 11-year-old son or my 9-year-old daughter who attended that vigil.

The curse of Matthew's death is easy to see. But what of the blessing? How can good come of hate, violence and death?

What blessings have the painful events of your life brought you? One of my colleagues says the only *real* growth in life comes disguised as pain or suffering. Most of my major lessons in life have come that way. Some people go as far as to say, "That which does not kill us makes us stronger." I find that statement hard to believe as I have witnessed many things that do not kill people, but surely cannot help make you stronger—I am not convinced that rape, incest or living through war has a consistent record of making people stronger; but I do believe that much of our growth as humans comes wearing the mask of pain and failure.

Perhaps Matthew Shepard was an angel, a guiding spirit to thousands—maybe millions of people throughout the United States and the world. In towns and cities throughout our country, anti-discrimination laws are beginning to include sexual orientation. Perhaps Matthew Shepard is the blessing, the angel that will propel this law into the books when it is put to vote in your community.

Everything is both blessing and curse. Examine your life. Can you see the blessings in the failures of your life? Can you see the curse in the successes you've had? Look closely at your life, your days, your gifts and the lessons you have learned. Of the lessons where you have learned the most, what was the precipitating factor that led to your growth?

Matthew Shepard has become a member of my family—one of the best teachers my children will ever have. He has taught my children that anger and hatred is wrong, even the anger and hatred they feel for the people who murdered Matthew. They learned that when they become violently angry they become nothing better than the killers of Matthew Shepard and the murderers and rapists of the world. They learned that they must turn the energy of their anger into productive, constructive, well-meaning actions that will not only neutralize the hatred caused by bigotry, but will also be a force toward eliminating it.

The blessing here is clear: The children of the world must work hard toward ending the kind of anger and hatred that has caused the deaths of all the Matthew Shepard's of the world.

29

There Are No Epiphanies

Sometimes I love doing therapy; sometimes it's just a job. I am certain this sentiment rings true for everyone who has a job that others see as glamorous or exciting. Being a psychologist is one of those jobs. People are always interested in my job, they want to hear something about it or they want to ask some kind of question. Often, they will look at me, and say, "Oh ... uh huh," when I tell them what I do. It's a commonly strange reaction; I get it all the time.

Sometimes, people will ask if I am *"analyzing them,"* and I tell them, "If you're not paying me, I'm not doing it!" It's weird how people react to the news of what I do for a living. Sometimes, when they are sure I am psychoanalyzing them, I have to ask them if their plumber friends come to their homes and start messing around under their sink, or if they know any electrician friends who come over to their homes just to screw around in their circuit box. People actually think therapists can read minds, and if we could, they think that theirs is so interesting that we'd rather do that than hang out and watch our kids play soccer. It can be both funny and annoying, depending on the person or the day.

Anyhow, sometimes, I love my job. It seems that mostly, I love it when I have a client who is ready to do his or her work. This past week that happened with Brianna when she came in to therapy, ready to look at herself and understand things about who and how she is (and has been) in a way she had not seen before. Brianna had been in therapy before, but this time, she was ready. It was truly a case of "when the student is ready the teacher will come."

Lucky for me, I just happened to be there when Brianna was ready.

The week before in her therapy hour I'd experienced a feeling of pressure in regards to her. It was not a new or a strange feeling, but it was still uncomfortable. It was the feeling that Brianna expected something magical to happen. That she had felt good about our previous sessions and she seemed to use this good feeling to lead her to expect that she was on the road to some incredible insight that would transform her life forever. As psychologists, we hate when this happens. This feeling is not unusual for first time patients, but for an "experienced" client, it is. Often, we have to teach clients about the therapy process—what it's like and how it's supposed to function. We teach that the responsibility is on the client, that it is our job to facilitate the process, not to find some magical cure; we leave magical cures to the medical doctors.

In this session with Brianna, I could see her hope growing. She appeared to think that, with my help, she was on the verge of some incredible epiphany, and I was taking her there. This is a dangerously seductive place for a therapist to allow him or herself to be and I could feel the pressure and the heat rising. I asked Brianna what she expected and what her hope for our therapy was. As with many clients, she said that she had been in therapy before and she was ready to understand herself in a new way. She said that maybe this time she would see what happened to her to cause her to struggle with finding intimacy throughout her life.

This caused me to tell her to stop. I asked her to stop talking and to take some time to listen. I asked her to re-learn about how therapy, life, and coming to understand ourselves really happen. It was not going to be good news for her. The news was simple to say, difficult to hear, even more difficult to apply.

"Brianna," I said, "There is no epiphany." Therapy, like life, is a process not an event. Rarely does someone walk into therapy and come out (in 45 minutes!) with a dramatic change in how they have seen themselves. Rarely does a person uncover the single event that has caused their pain. I ask my clients not to come to me expecting that this will happen, because it doesn't. It would be nice if it did (maybe), but understanding oneself is not that simple, and behavioral change is even more difficult than gaining the insight of the minor epiphanies that therapy sometimes provides.

So, relax as you go through the *therapy* of life. Don't be disappointed when the epiphany doesn't come. Look for the little lessons and understand there is much more to seeing the process of life than waiting for the significant insightful events.

Since there is really only one *"getting there"* (death), take some time today to enjoy the ride.

30

Checking the Mail

Some people just *love* getting the mail. Getting mail is their favorite thing in life; they wait eagerly for it everyday. They love mail. This can be especially true with email.

In one part of town, the mail may come early in the morning, sometimes it comes in the late afternoon; sometimes it comes at noon, sometimes it comes at night. The fact is that the mail can come any time of the day or night. If you are one of those people who *love* the mail, live for the mail, and the mail can come in at any time, you probably check it *all the time*. First thing in the morning and hundreds of times during the day—until the mail comes in, you check. This is how email often is, it comes in intermittently, and unpredictably. If you are waiting for an important email from someone you are dying to hear from, you will check your computer all the time.

In another part of town the mail comes in at the same time every day. If you live here and you *love* the mail and the letter carrier brings the mail at noon every day, you probably check the mail at noon, or perhaps you get there and wait at 11:55 am. You just *love* the mail. If your email came in every day at noon, and you REALLY loved your email, you would probably check right at noon, or slightly before.

Wanting and waiting for a great relationship can be like this too, and almost everyone I meet wants to find a great relationship. Kendra and Chris were two such women who came to sit on my couch. Here's their story:

Kendra *loves* her father. Sometimes, he is the greatest father in the world. He comes home and plays with Kendra, reads to her, gives her a bath, kicks a ball, takes her for ice cream. Kendra *loves* when her father acts like the best father in the world.

Sometimes, Kendra's father is not so great; frankly, he's downright awful. He comes home in a bad mood, he complains and yells, slams doors, and is mean to everyone, including Kendra. Kendra still *loves* her unpredictable father. Each night, when he comes home, Kendra anxiously waits by the door to see which father will come home.

Chris also *loves* her father. Every time Chris's father comes home, he is the same. He kisses the family hello, reads the daily paper, eats dinner, talks pleasantly about his day, says goodnight, and goes to bed. Chris just *loves* her father, too. At night, when he comes home, you can usually find Chris doing her homework, reading or playing. Chris's father has to go find her; she never waits anxiously to see which father comes home.

Kendra and Chris come to counseling as adults. They come for very different reasons.

Kendra seems to keep finding herself in volatile relationships; she wonders why she keeps getting into relationships with people who treat her poorly at times. Chris, on the other hand, can't seem to find any excitement in life. Her relationships seem calm, almost boring.

What happened to Kendra and Chris? Will they find relationships like this forever?

The most powerful reinforcer of human behavior seems to be intermittent reinforcement. Kendra keeps finding relationships that alternate between wonderful, loving and fun to occasionally unhealthy, scary and unpredictable. She initially falls in love with the "prince" who seems to have a tendency to turn into a "frog." This pattern of romantic relationships seems to find her every time. She finds herself in relationships that are sometimes wonderful and loving, and other times unstable and unforgiving. Then, because she craves a perfect loving relationship, just like the person who loves the *mail*, she discovers herself "checking" for the *mail* all the time. And she finds herself stuck in a dysfunctional, sometimes harmful relationship. She finds that sometimes the *mail* is in, sometimes it isn't, but Kendra keeps checking. She becomes obsessed with the looking; the people in her life tend to be like this too, they get their *buzz* by checking to see if the mail is in. Sometimes it is, sometimes, it isn't. There is an excitement that comes with the adventure of trying to find the mail. There is also a price that Kendra pays for this pattern. Kendra must decide if the price she pays is worth the benefits she gets. When the relationship is good, it is VERY good and Kendra craves this kind of *mail* (male?). But when it is bad, it is VERY bad.

Kendra asks me why she keeps going back to relationships that cause her emotional (and sometimes physical) pain. I tell her that it's because she loves when the *mail* comes in. And sometimes it does, even though, most times, it doesn't. Actually, it usually only comes in once a day, but this is enough to keep her checking. It takes an awful lot to break this pattern. The behavior becomes very strong, and addictive. In gambling casinos the slot machine rooms always seem to draw the biggest, most consistent crowds.

Chris never plays the slots; she may even forget to check her mail. She wants to know what she can do to get some excitement into her life. Chris wants to know if Kendra's life is better than her life. She sees the pain that Kendra is in, but she also sees the joy she gets when the relationship is great and the mail (figuratively) comes in.

Kendra sees the calm that Chris appears to have and wonders if being *that* way would be better for her. Checking for the payoff in life can get tiring. As I sit with Kendra and Chris something about grass being greener comes to mind, and I wonder, along with them, if people can ever really change their lifelong patterns in relationships.

Kendra wanted the excitement Chris seemed to find, and Chris wanted the stability that Kendra was tired of. Each of these patients wanted a relationship that was fulfilling, exciting, and fun. Their patterns of reinforcement from childhood were vastly different and this difference has led them to seek out satisfying relationships with very different kinds of partners. They wanted similar experiences in their romantic relationships and sought them out employing different methods. Both want healthy, loving, secure relationships that can offer them the love they want (and need) in a romantic partner. Kendra will continue to get a buzz from checking for the mail, and Chris will continue to be bored by knowing exactly when it comes in. Both women will have to find a combination of healthy reward systems so that they can get what they want—and perhaps by seeing what the other has they can find ways to combine their two patterns to get more of what they want.

As you explore the kind of relationships you want, which pattern do you find yourself drawn to? If you were on my couch I'd want to ask: "How's that working for you? And what are you ready to change?"

31

Life is Like a Lava Lamp

Lava lamps were very popular when I was in college. Their calm, flowing motion represented the way we hoped to feel, but rarely ever did. When the light heats the lava to a warm temperature, the lava flows gently, rhythmically ... the flow of the lamp is soothing. Life can be like that sometimes. Other times, life is like a lava lamp when it is all shook up. Have you ever seen a lava lamp when it has been shaken? Don't do it—believe me about this one.

Jack Rider was my first college roommate and a casual friend from my hometown. Jack had a lava lamp. He brought it with him to college in 1974. It was red. Sometimes we would sit around the room and turn out all the lights except the "black light" and the lava lamp. Man, I'll tell you, we had the coolest room in the dorm. The lava lamp would flow and the black light would illuminate the posters in our room, Jimi Hendrix, The Doors, and some psychedelic mind-tripping posters came to life as 1970's rock would blare from the stereo.

When Jack would leave the room to go out with his friends he would often say, "C'mon guys, don't mess with my lava lamp. It gets really messed up if you shake it." We never knew what he meant, and we didn't take him too seriously about his lamp, or anything else.

None of my friends liked Jack very much. He wasn't a very happy person and he was easy to dislike. He was always complaining about something and had a permanent scowl on his face that made him look angry, even when he wasn't. His eyes were crooked too, with one 'lazy' eye that drifted toward his nose when he looked at you. I'm embarrassed to say that he was easy to make fun of—and he probably knew we were doing it. You might know someone like Jack; he was a disagreeable sort who didn't have very many real friends.

One night when Jack was out, my friends and I were feeling especially playful and we began challenging each other to shake his lava lamp. Nobody wanted to do it, and even though we didn't like Jack, we did like his lamp. We must've been really egging each other on that night; boys can get pretty rowdy doing this, challenging each other's manhood with name-calling and dares; you probably know how a group of friends can get when the anxiety builds in the moment. The tension built up with an odd combination of laughter and anxiety as we continued to push each other not to be cowards. And then the tension got released when—well, I'm sure you can guess what happened next. Somebody (I swear it wasn't me) shook Jack's lava lamp. The lava gel broke into thousands of tiny pieces and we knew in that exact moment why Jack had warned us not to shake his precious lamp. It looked awful as the gentle flow of lava turned instantly into a mix of oil, water and tiny (non-flowing) pieces of gel that, minutes ago, used to be so soothing. It looked awful. Of course, we laughed our asses off at first. It was really funny. Funny in the nervous kind of way that causes you to laugh uncontrollably, like after you almost get into a car accident but don't. Funny in the way that makes you laugh hysterically when you see somebody fall but not really get hurt. Funny like "Oh hell, whatta-we-gonna-do-now?" Funny like your parents just told you to quit laughing in church. It was funny in a way that may not really be funny—the kind of humorous moment when you are overtaken by that odd mix of emotion that straddles the line somewhere between amusement, hysteria and fear.

When Jack came back to the room, none of us were there. He must have been in shock when he spotted that mutiny of gel. He'd told us hundreds of times not to shake his lamp. I'm certain it wasn't funny to him. Later, when Jack asked me who had shaken his lamp I acted as if I were seeing the tiny pieces of lava gel for the first time. Jack's face was more sad than angry. It was the first time I had seen him as a person, with feelings and reactions like most people feel when something bad happens to someone they care about.

Jack was right, we shouldn't have shaken his lava lamp, it was wrong. None of us really stopped to think about Jack that night. We knew he wouldn't be happy, but we probably didn't care. Jack never looked like he had feelings or emotions like the rest of us. That's probably why we never felt close to him or liked him very much. Seeing Jack *feel* an emotion other than anger seemed to make him more real to me that day; he became almost likeable that morning. Shaking Jack's lava lamp was both a crisis and an opportunity, and it taught me a number of valuable lessons about life and people. It taught me that when people show sadness or hurt they become more real, even people I don't like very much.

We all learned another lesson that day, a funny lesson. When Jack asked who had shaken his lava lamp he discovered something many of us don't learn until we are parents. He learned that the person who shook his lamp was the same person who does everything bad in my house—both growing up and today (and probably in your house too): it was **NOBODY!**

Yes, it was *Nobody*, Nobody did it. Nobody does everything bad at my house and Nobody was there that night to shake Jack Rider's lava lamp.

The lamp was a mess, and this crisis led us to be closer and see each other more clearly as human beings with real emotions. It took literally weeks for the lamp's heat to return the lava flow to normal. Just like life. As I examine my life, and the lives of the people who come to me for help I can see that when the lava in our lamps gets too shook up, it breaks into a million pieces and we need the warmth of those who love us to help us flow right again. I think this is true of most people. It was true for Jack and is true for me. In everyone's life there are events that shake the lava in his or her lamps and at those times it is essential for each of us to find someone who will help us return to our normal flow, someone to give us some heat, some light to soothe our pain when we feel like we've been broken into thousands of tiny pieces.

So be careful when Nobody is around, watch out for your lava lamp or the lava lamp that is you, because when it gets shaken too hard, it takes a long time to flow right again—sometimes it never does. The lessons here are many, about Jack, his pain, how he showed it and how he held it in. There are lessons about having fun, reconnecting, seeing hurt and taking responsibility. The lesson I learned is to watch out for *Nobody*, especially when Nobody is you or one of your closest friends and he or she is lurking in your life ready to shake you up.

32

The Times, They Are A Changin'

There were certain things my parents would never have said or done around their parents, my grandparents. There were certain things I would have never said or done around my parents. It seems that with each passing generation, children become more comfortable being "inappropriate" around their parents than the generation before them. I know that I have said and done more inappropriate things around my parents than my parents would have done around theirs. I never would have cursed around my parents, but today, my teenage children hardly think any more about dropping certain swear words around me than they worry about dropping their dirty laundry in their rooms! I go a little crazy when people say that things aren't any different today than in the past. Things *are* different today than in the past and to think they are not is naïve.

One night, a few years ago while we were eating dinner our eleven-year-old son asked, with a giggle, *"What's Viagra?"*

I told him that Viagra is a medicine used to help men with their erections. He giggled again, but seemed to understand. He said some kids were talking about it at school, saying that they were going to give some to the principal, but he really didn't know why this was supposed to be funny.

Upon hearing this, Rachel, our nine year-old, asked, *"What's an erection?"*

Her mother piped up quickly, *"Nothing,"* and she tried to change to the subject.

I jumped in and said casually, *"An erection is when a man's penis gets big. Viagra is used when that doesn't happen the way it's suppose to."* I think it's better to answer our children's questions rather than leave them to go someplace else to ask them—or worse, leave them to imagine that it's such a bad thing to ask or talk about that they internalize this 'bad feeling/thought' and come to believe that there may be something wrong with them for asking or thinking about it.

Kids today hear the darndest things. Most kids can read by first grade and with most newspapers seemingly written on a sixth-grade level they can figure a lot out. So, they see things in the newspaper that they can read, and since we encourage them to ask questions about what they're learning and reading they want to know what words like "r-a-p-e" are and what it means if they see a newspaper that says that someone got "raped." They see that someone was charged with sexual harassment or that some teacher sexually molested a kid in her or his class and they wonder, 'what is sexual harassment?' They hear on the news that the president had sex with an intern using cigars and they wonder how that can be (I think we all wondered about that).

It's no wonder that kids talk and act differently today than our grandparents did, our parents did and we did. We can practically guarantee that our kid's kids will act differently too.

When I was about nine years old, I served hot dogs and drinks to people at the weekly bingo night. I worked for free, received some tips and was lucky if I made ten dollars for the entire night. Actually, ten dollars would have been a great night. Anyhow, I recall talking to an older woman (most of the bingo players were old people) and telling her that my teacher was pregnant. Well you would have thought I was telling her about erections! She almost fell out of her chair. Later that night my mother taught me one would never say the word "pregnant" in that woman's youth. It just wasn't done. They had cute little expressions back then; "She was in a family way" was probably the most popular.

The times have changed. Some would say for the better, some would say for the worse. The way my kids talk around me is incredibly different than how I would've spoken around my parents. I never would have thought it was ok to curse around my parents until I was at least driving age, and then it was only an occasional "shit" or "damn" or "hell." We'd never say those *other* words.

Sometimes, I wonder what is coming down the road for the next generation of kids. The way our kids talk and fight with us, the way they tattoo and pierce their bodies, I'm guessing there's not much left to do in this direction. Heck, what's left for our children to use to rebel? Being good? Or perhaps pulling out guns and knives and using them when they are mad or rebelling?

We grew our hair long. The generation before ours rolled cigarettes up in their T-shirt sleeves. Today, my kids have different color hair every week, pierced tongues and tattoos. Bob Dylan said, *"The times, they are a changin.'"* I guess he was right. Pretending things aren't really any different today isn't very helpful. So, if the times are changin', and they are different, our only choice as adults seems to be either to change with them, or get out of the way.

I'm not ready to move over. So I think I'll listen to the new music, check out a new magazine, talk to my kids, and see where I fit in, see what I can learn, and see what they can teach me. If the only constant is change, and things keep changing, I better find some way to make peace with the changes and stop pretending that things aren't really that different than when I was a kid, because they are. Holding onto the past can't all be bad, but holding on by pretending that things haven't changed can't be good. It will leave me out of step with the culture in which I live and the people who surround me, namely, my kids and their kids and a generation of people who will someday get teased about *their* old-fashioned ways, just like I teased my parents and my parents teased theirs.

The times, they are a changin' and it's up to me to figure out what I'm gonna do about that.

33

The Ghosts of Christmas Past

It's early November, just past Halloween, the unofficial start of the holiday season. I think it's time to stop complaining that the holiday season starts too early, this is when it begins in the United States, let's get used to it. This is when it starts every year! I've even heard a Christmas song the day after Halloween. 'Happens every year.

Susan came to therapy to begin to deal with her ghosts of Christmas past—Susan came early, to avoid the Christmas rush. Every year at this time many of my patients will want to talk about the holiday traumas in their lives. For many therapists, the holiday season brings a daily crowd of Christmas-fearing souls; it does for me.

Susan's story was not unusual; Christmas brings with it the pain of childhood in a way few other memories can, and she cried easily just sitting in the office reflecting on her Christmas-times past. She wanted to help her own two daughters avoid the pain she remembers, she wanted to help her children have Christmases that are great.

Her children will probably struggle with the holiday season when they get older too, whether Susan helps them have good Christmases or not. The holiday season is just good business if your business is toys, clothes, cologne or providing therapy. What is going on here?

Well, the toys, clothes and cologne are fairly obvious, so I won't go into why those businesses boom right after Halloween. But what happens to people that leads them to therapy? Susan even said that her memories of Christmas were good; she didn't have the stories some of her friends had about drunken parties, family fights, or not getting what she wanted. She mostly remembered that the holiday season was joyful and fun, yet every year since she has been an adult she gets a little down right after Thanksgiving. She claimed it seems to be happening earlier and earlier every year.

This week, in therapy, she asked about this phenomenon. She claimed she sees it in others too; remember, misery loves company that's also miserable. Unfortunately, people often "put on their happy faces" during the holiday season. As a result, many people wonder why no one else seems to struggle like *they* do (this is a concern all year long for people in therapy). Many clients tell me, "Everybody else seems so damn happy, then they ask what is *wrong* with them."

Susan wanted to know what was going on with her. She wanted to know if there was some deep psychological reason that led her to feel downhearted every Christmas. She thought, like many patients, if only she knew *why* she was down she would cease to be depressed—which is true sometimes, but usually not.

We began talking about the "problems" that are magnified during the holiday season—the ones that people often have all year long, but become exacerbated during the holidays. There are the obvious ones: money is tight all year long, tighter at Christmas (you just **have** to spend more); people are *forced* to spent more time with family members, even the ones you get to avoid most of the year. Our time is usually more rushed as we try to cram things into each day while none of the other "things" go away (cooking, cleaning, laundry, work etc.); often, our alcohol and drug use is up during the holidays, and while we'd like to think these substances lead us to have more fun, they often lead us to feel cranky and irritable. Those are the *normal* stressors, the obvious ones, and the ones we're all mostly aware of. But one particular stressor appears to be the most painful underlying cause of the holiday blues. I call it *'The Ghost of Christmas Past.'*

Susan has fond memories of her childhood Christmases. Many people do. This confused Susan when, at twenty-five or so, she began to feel down right after Thanksgiving and getting earlier every year. Susan, and maybe you too, had the chance to live with the magic of Christmas from the ages of two or three until the age of eight or nine. This is approximately five, maybe six years. Five, maybe six years, of pure innocence. Maybe you got to experience unadulterated innocence, magic, joy, mystery, love and people giving things (including toys) to you. There were lights, music, people, smells, sights, and things. There was a sensory overload placed upon your five-through-nine-year-old self that will never be found again. The magic of Christmas is something so overwhelming, few words can describe all that it means (meant) to your little innocent, child-like self. And this magic, once exposed, can never be captured again.

My job is to help people see and understand this phenomenon, to help Susan and others gain the insight necessary to help decrease the depression, to attempt to find some way to regain the innocence lost and make the facsimile as close as possible to the childhood experience of magic that was left in Christmas past.

The phenomenon is easy to understand if you think of the magic that the Christmas season is. The magic of Christmas between the ages of five and nine is that you don't know the "trick." If you were David Copperfield's assistant and YOU got to see how he does his magic—if you got to see how the trick works—do you think the magic would be as magical? It wouldn't. Christmas season is like that. Once you see how Copperfield gets out of the box he's locked up in, it never looks the same as when you used to watch it from the audience. Christmas is different when you're a spectator than when you're the magician.

This is the curse of Christmas past. Susan, and I, and maybe you, have both clear and vague memories of this incredible time. For the remainder of our lives we have an unconscious desire to re-capture the magic of this five-year time period of our lives. And if you really want to analyze it, you will see that it wasn't really even five years, it was only five seasons. We essentially have five—maybe six—incredible, great, magical, truly fantastic Christmases in our lives ... then, for the rest of our lives, we try to grab the magic of those five Christmases. But we never can; innocence lost is not easy to get back. Having children of our own helps, but is mostly a reasonable facsimile of our own experience as children.

You will never see Christmas again like you saw it when you were five—so before you get depressed this year, consider that. The magic won't be the same—it's impossible to capture—but it doesn't have to be depressing once you learn what changed. You can help yourself, but you better start early this year ... it's already past Halloween.

34

Yadda-Yadda-Yadda

Certain behaviors that people engage in are unintentionally humorous. Some people are just downright funny and they don't even know it. My brother Mitchell was always one of these people. As a sign of how healthy he became, as he got older he learned to laugh with us as we laughed at him for the many speaking faux pas he'd make. Norm Crosby, a comedian, even made an entire career out of malapropisms.

One of my favorite examples of unintended humor is when people use inaccurate words or "filler" phrases. I do it a lot too. I think English teachers and wordsmiths are the only ones who don't do this; I sometimes chuckle at how annoyed they seem to get when language gets twisted up and used incorrectly. Some people have such a command over the language that nobody knows what they are talking about half the time. Other people are not so good at using words and they say things that either don't mean anything or words that don't even exist.

Jargon, slang, and idioms are so popular in the English language that often, it is difficult for foreigners to learn to speak it or understand it until they have lived here for a while. I know the same is true for Americans who go to another country to learn a new language. Texting, instant messaging and email seem to have added to this problem.

One of today's most popular expressions is the use of, *"Yadda-yadda-yadda."* This phrase seems to have replaced *"blah, blah, blah,"* when we don't want to tell the rest of a story.

One of my favorites is when people say, *"To make a long story short."* You know it's probably already too late when they say this. One client I had used to say, *"This, that, and the other thing."* He sprinkled it throughout his stories often. One session I counted him saying it, and he repeated the phrase 47 times—really!

Saying, *"… if you will"* at the end of a sentence always baffled me. How about when people say: *"To be perfectly honest with you,"* or, *"… to tell you the truth,"* as if they weren't going to be honest with you unless they said that. I also like it when they say, *"I'll be honest with you,"* at the beginning of a sentence. Sometimes, these same people will end a sentence with: *"… you know what I'm saying?"* I always want to say *"no"* when they ask that. One woman I was working with ended **every** sentence with that phrase. You know what I'm saying?

I particularly like when people use words that don't exist but that have been used so much, few people realize they are not real words. For example, there is no word *"heighth."* Just because there is a word *"width"* doesn't mean there has to be the word heighth—there isn't! *"Weighth"* isn't a word either; weight is. Weighth isn't as popular as heighth, but it can't be far behind, can it? One client of mine used to tell me how *"voictrous"* he was, I think he meant boisterous, only better. I used to get so *"flustrated"* with him for saying this non-word.

Another favorite of mine is when people mix metaphors … I actually try to do this myself sometimes, just for the fun of it … one client of mine was particularly fond of saying, *"taking things to the tilt!"* instead of taking them to the hilt. (Not that I know what the hilt is!)

People often say, *"... so forth and so on,"* at the end of a story. I guess that's better than hearing the rest of it; I mean if you can get it from those five words, why hear the rest? I think "so forth and so on" is closely related to *"so on and so forth,"* you can probably use those interchangeably. You may also hear *"what not,"* at the end of a sentence, I don't think I understand that one at all. What do you think of *"such and such,"* or *"thus and such,"* (which must be first cousins of each other in the speech world)?

Sometimes, just for fun, I try to see how many filler phrases and fake words I can use. Just for the fun of it, try to see how many you can use. Here are some suggestions for you to put into your day today.

Have fun with words today, figure out how many non-words and meaningless phrases you can come up with and share them in your regular speaking patterns. It's a game you can get your friends to join you in and you can have lots of fun.

To tell you the truth, irregardless of his heighth, which was short, he was very voictrous in his discussion, but he always made a long story short, by saying so forth and so on, you know what I mean, he always said, "Yadda yadda yadda," you know what I'm saying?

Of course you do.

978-0-595-47362-5
0-595-47362-8